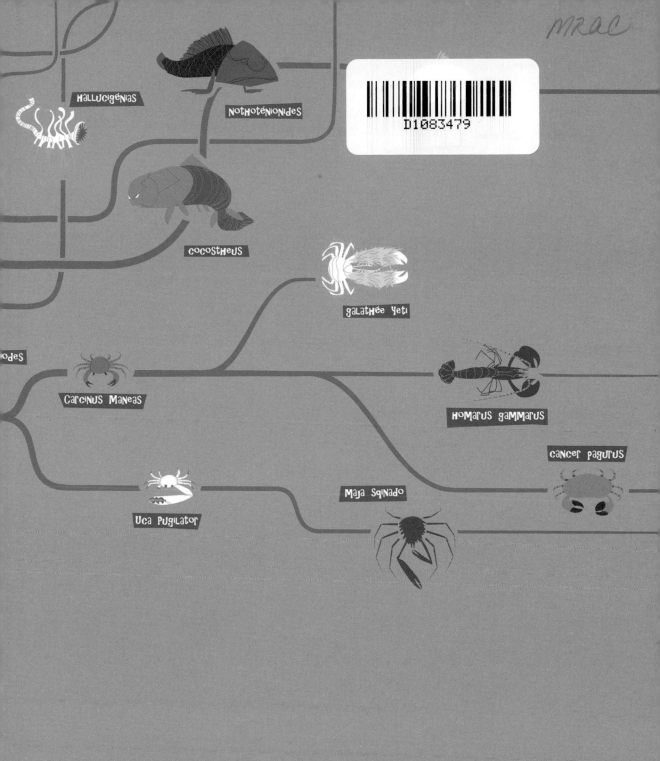

HaLLUCigéNiaS

NothoténioNides

cocostHeUS

galatHée Yeti

odes

CarciNUS MaNeaS

HoMarUS gaMMarUS

cancer PagUrUS

Uca PUgiLator

Maja SqiNado

THE MARCH OF THE CRABS

THE REVOLUTION OF THE CRABS

Published by
ARCHAIA™

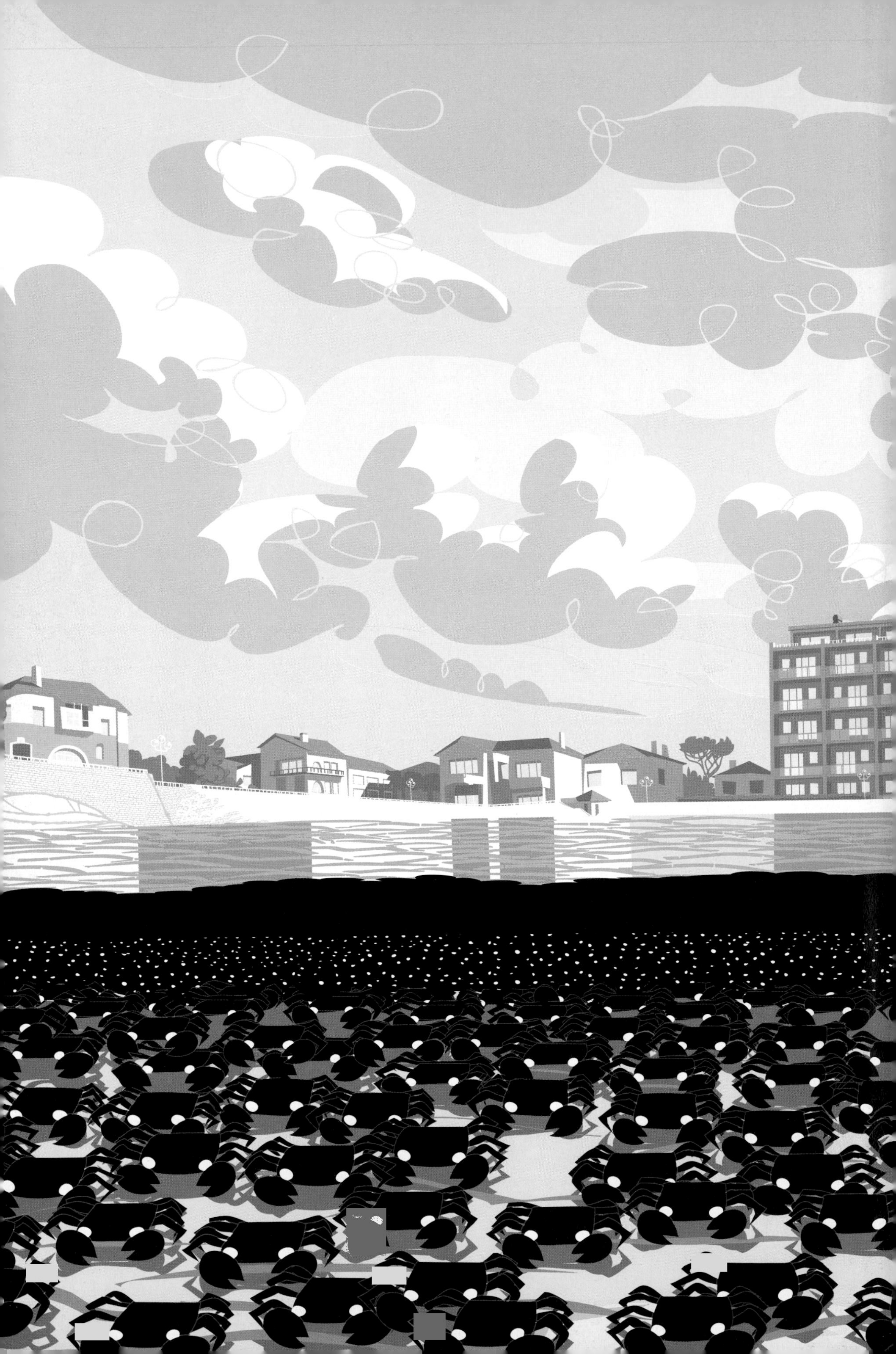

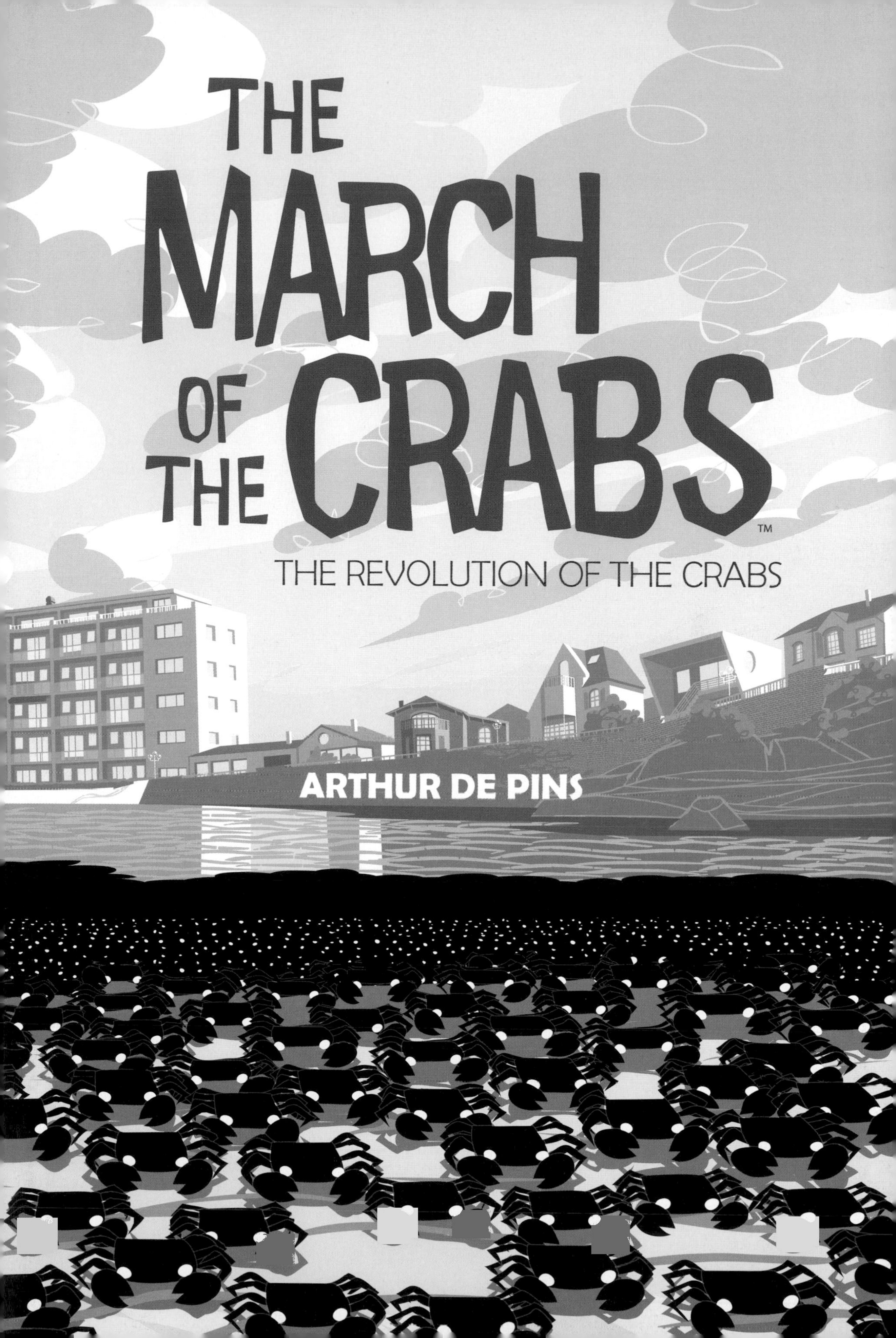
THE MARCH OF THE CRABS™
THE REVOLUTION OF THE CRABS
ARTHUR DE PINS

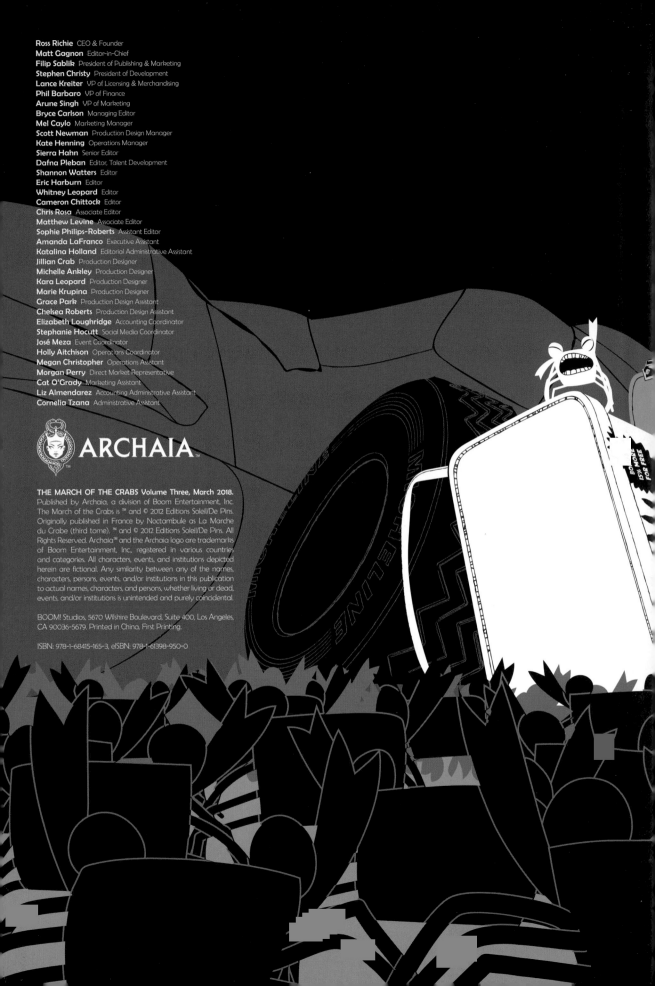

ARCHAIA

THE MARCH OF THE CRABS Volume Three, March 2018.
Published by Archaia, a division of Boom Entertainment, Inc.
The March of the Crabs is ™ and © 2012 Editions Soleil/De Pins.
Originally published in France by Noctambule as La Marche
du Crabe (third tome). ™ and © 2012 Editions Soleil/De Pins. All
Rights Reserved. Archaia™ and the Archaia logo are trademarks
of Boom Entertainment, Inc., registered in various countries
and categories. All characters, events, and institutions depicted
herein are fictional. Any similarity between any of the names,
characters, persons, events, and/or institutions in this publication
to actual names, characters, and persons, whether living or dead,
events, and/or institutions is unintended and purely coincidental.

BOOM! Studios, 5670 Wilshire Boulevard, Suite 400, Los Angeles,
CA 90036-5679. Printed in China. First Printing.

ISBN: 978-1-68415-165-3, eISBN: 978-1-61398-950-0

Written and illustrated by
ARTHUR DE PINS

Translated by
EDWARD GAUVIN

Lettered by
DERON BENNETT

FRENCH EDITION

Editor
CLOTILDE VU

Designed by
DIDIER GONORD and **ADELINE RICHET**

ENGLISH EDITION

Designed by
JILLIAN CRAB

Editors
CAMERON CHITTOCK
SIERRA HAHN

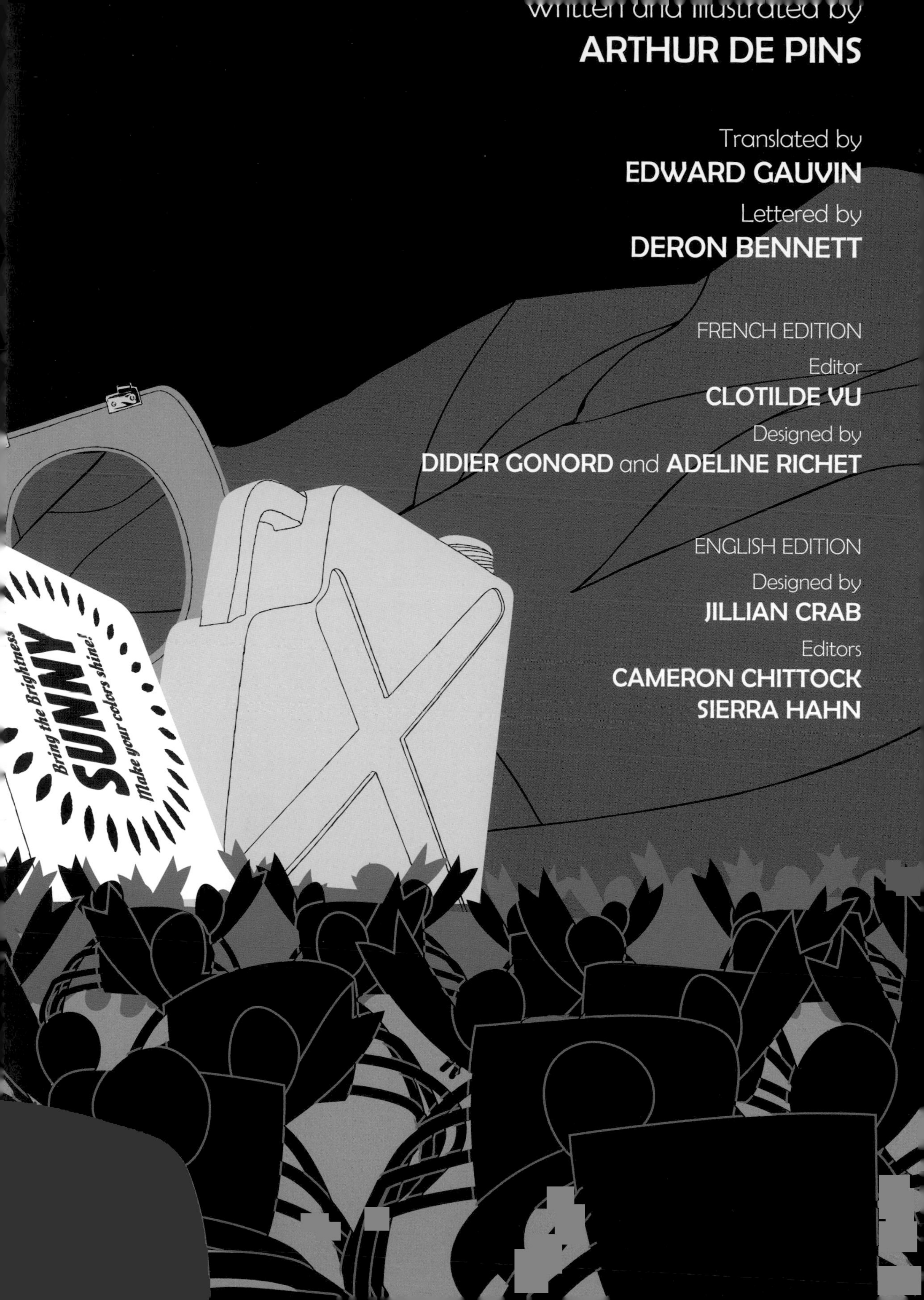
Bring the Brightness
SUNNY
Make your colors shine!

This trilogy is dedicated to Captain Erwan Donnelly.

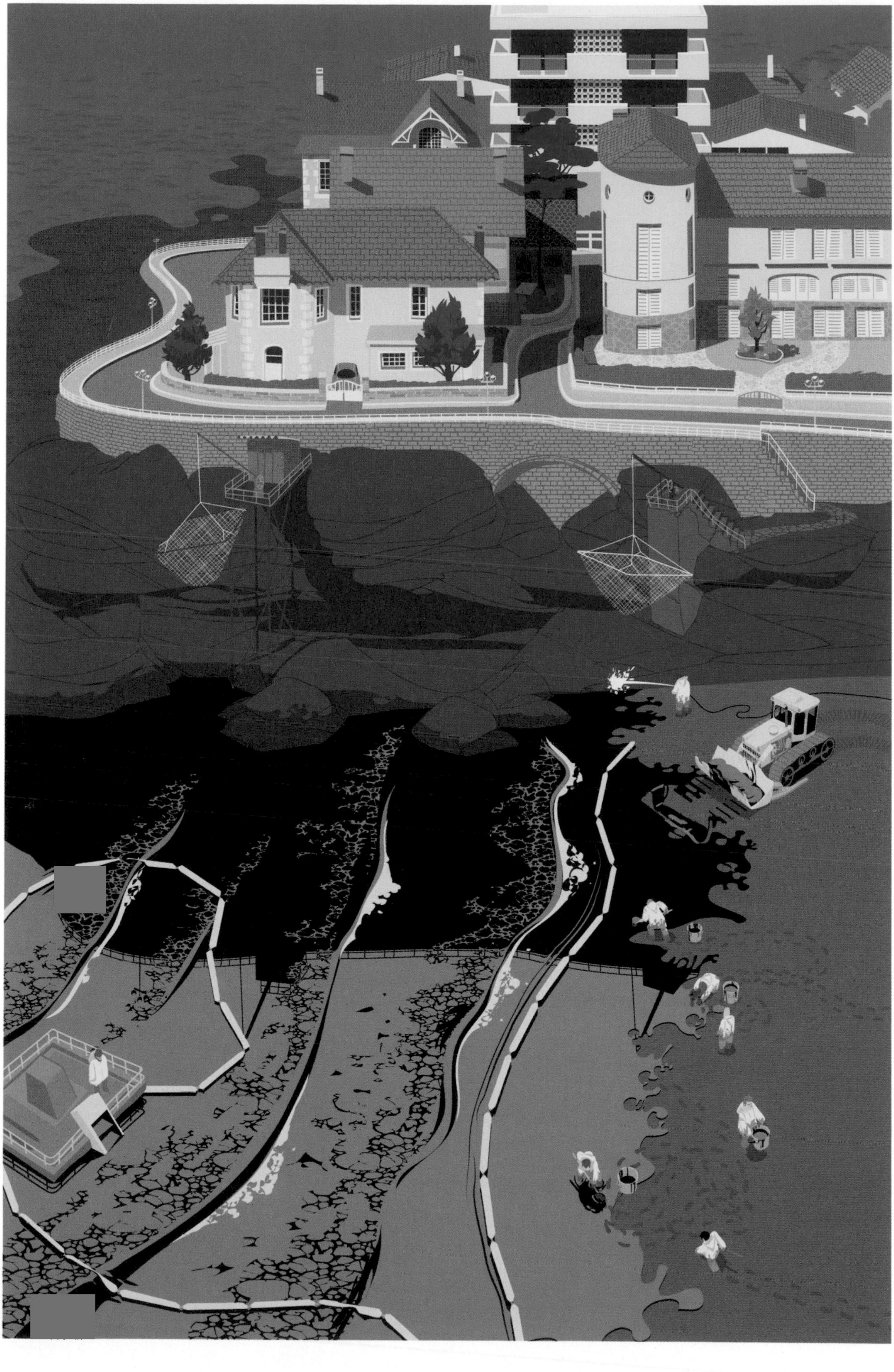

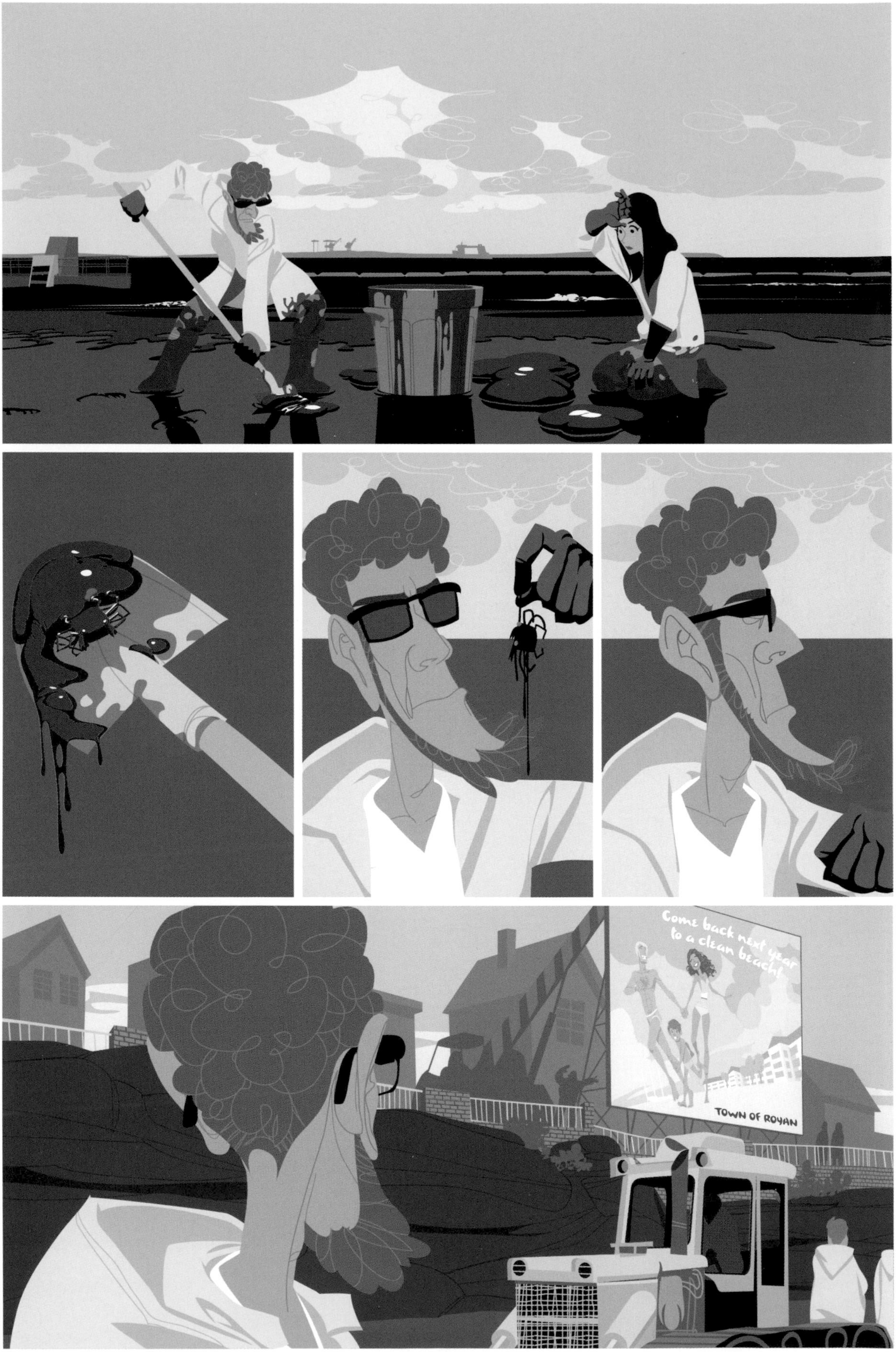
Come back next year to a clean beach!
TOWN OF ROYAN

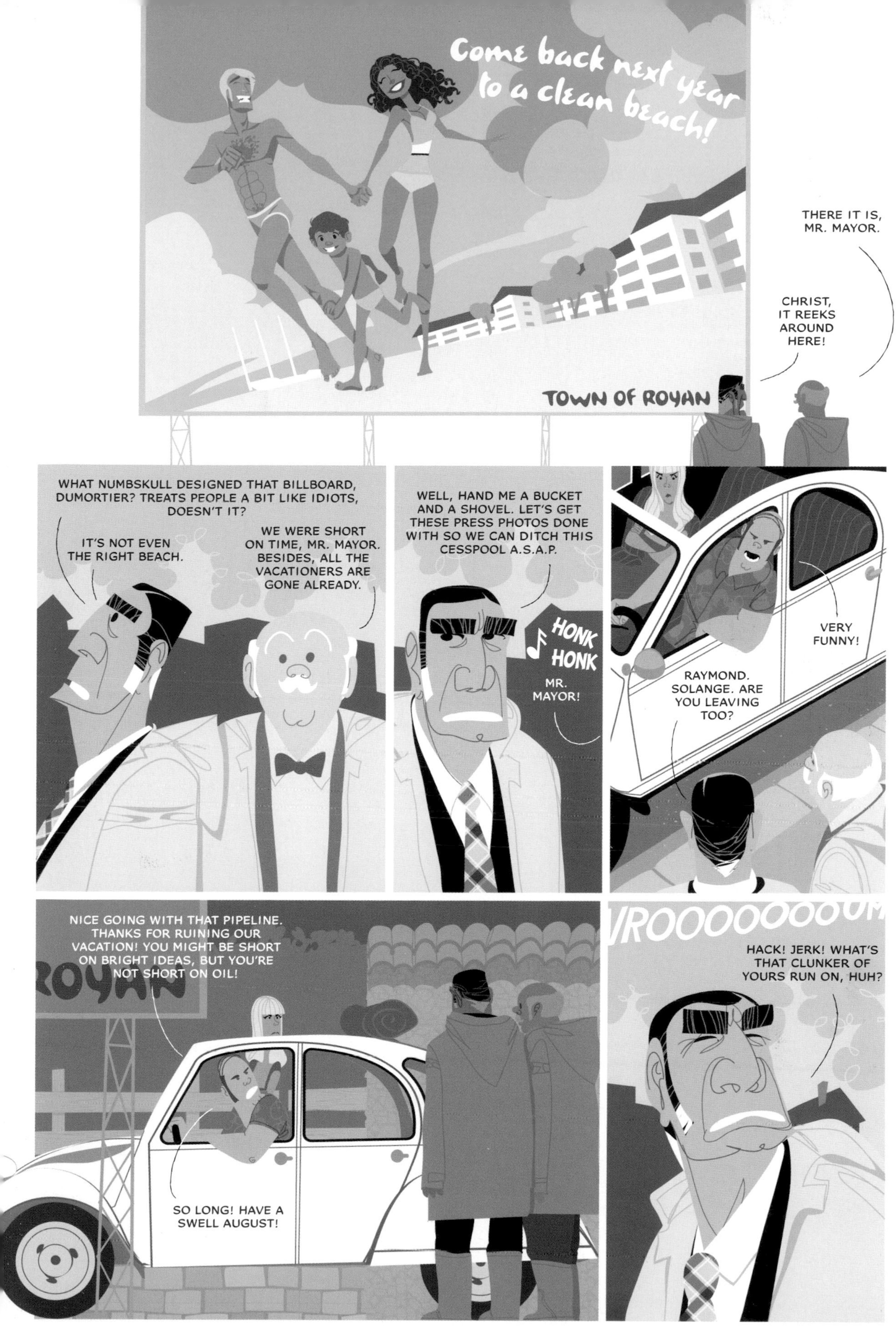
Come back next year to a clean beach!
TOWN OF ROYAN
THERE IT IS, MR. MAYOR.
CHRIST, IT REEKS AROUND HERE!
WHAT NUMBSKULL DESIGNED THAT BILLBOARD, DUMORTIER? TREATS PEOPLE A BIT LIKE IDIOTS, DOESN'T IT?
IT'S NOT EVEN THE RIGHT BEACH.
WE WERE SHORT ON TIME, MR. MAYOR. BESIDES, ALL THE VACATIONERS ARE GONE ALREADY.
WELL, HAND ME A BUCKET AND A SHOVEL. LET'S GET THESE PRESS PHOTOS DONE WITH SO WE CAN DITCH THIS CESSPOOL A.S.A.P.
HONK HONK
MR. MAYOR!
RAYMOND. SOLANGE. ARE YOU LEAVING TOO?
VERY FUNNY!
NICE GOING WITH THAT PIPELINE. THANKS FOR RUINING OUR VACATION! YOU MIGHT BE SHORT ON BRIGHT IDEAS, BUT YOU'RE NOT SHORT ON OIL!
SO LONG! HAVE A SWELL AUGUST!
VROOOOOOOOUM
HACK! JERK! WHAT'S THAT CLUNKER OF YOURS RUN ON, HUH?

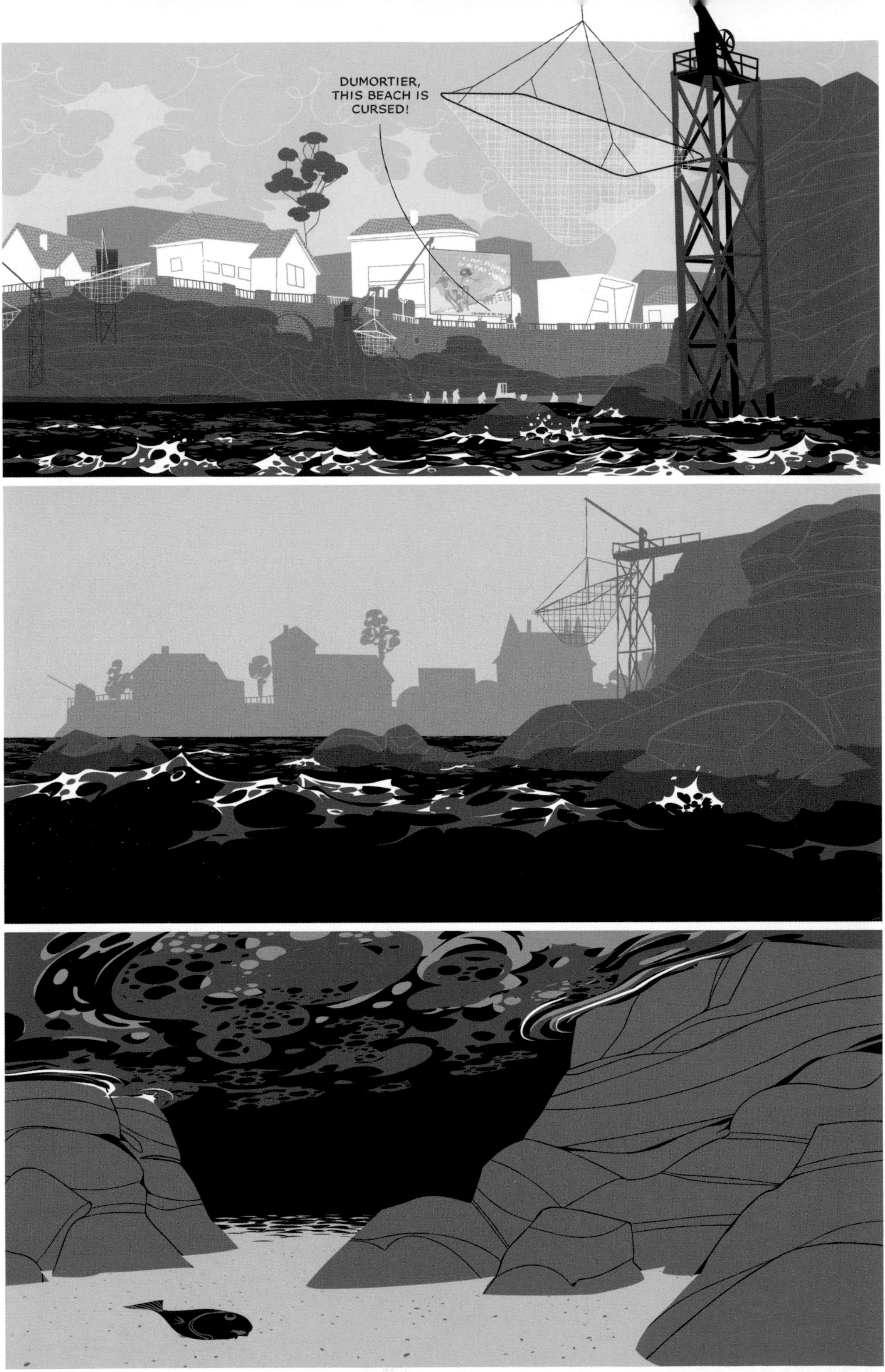
DUMORTIER, THIS BEACH IS CURSED!

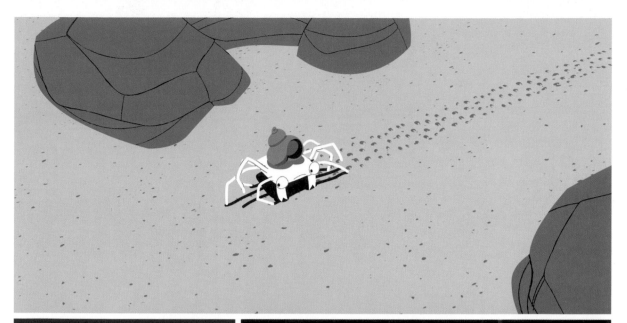

FASTER, YOU PACK OF SISSIES!

I SEE ANYONE STOP, I'LL LOP OFF THEIR CLAW!

AND DON'T JUST DROP FOOD AT THE **FOOT** OF THE HEAP. YOU PUT IT **ON TOP.** I WANT TO SEE A MOUNTAIN OF CHOW!

POUF!

HEY, YOU!

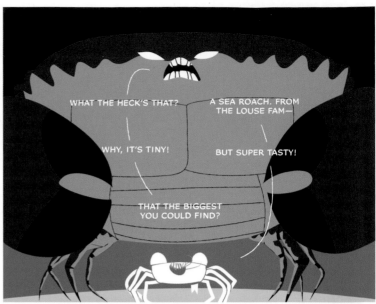

WHAT THE HECK'S THAT?

WHY, IT'S TINY!

THAT THE BIGGEST YOU COULD FIND?

A SEA ROACH. FROM THE LOUSE FAM—

BUT SUPER TASTY!

HEY, YOU THINK THIS IS EASY WITH JUST ONE CLAW?

YOU ATE THE OTHER ONE, IN CASE YOU FORGOT!

POW!

GO FIND ME SOMETHING ELSE!

OWWIEE!

POOF!

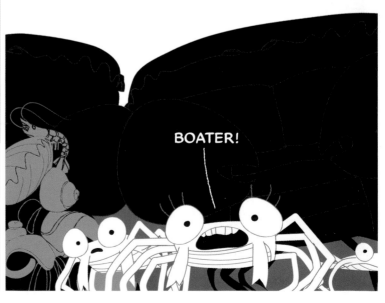

BOATER!

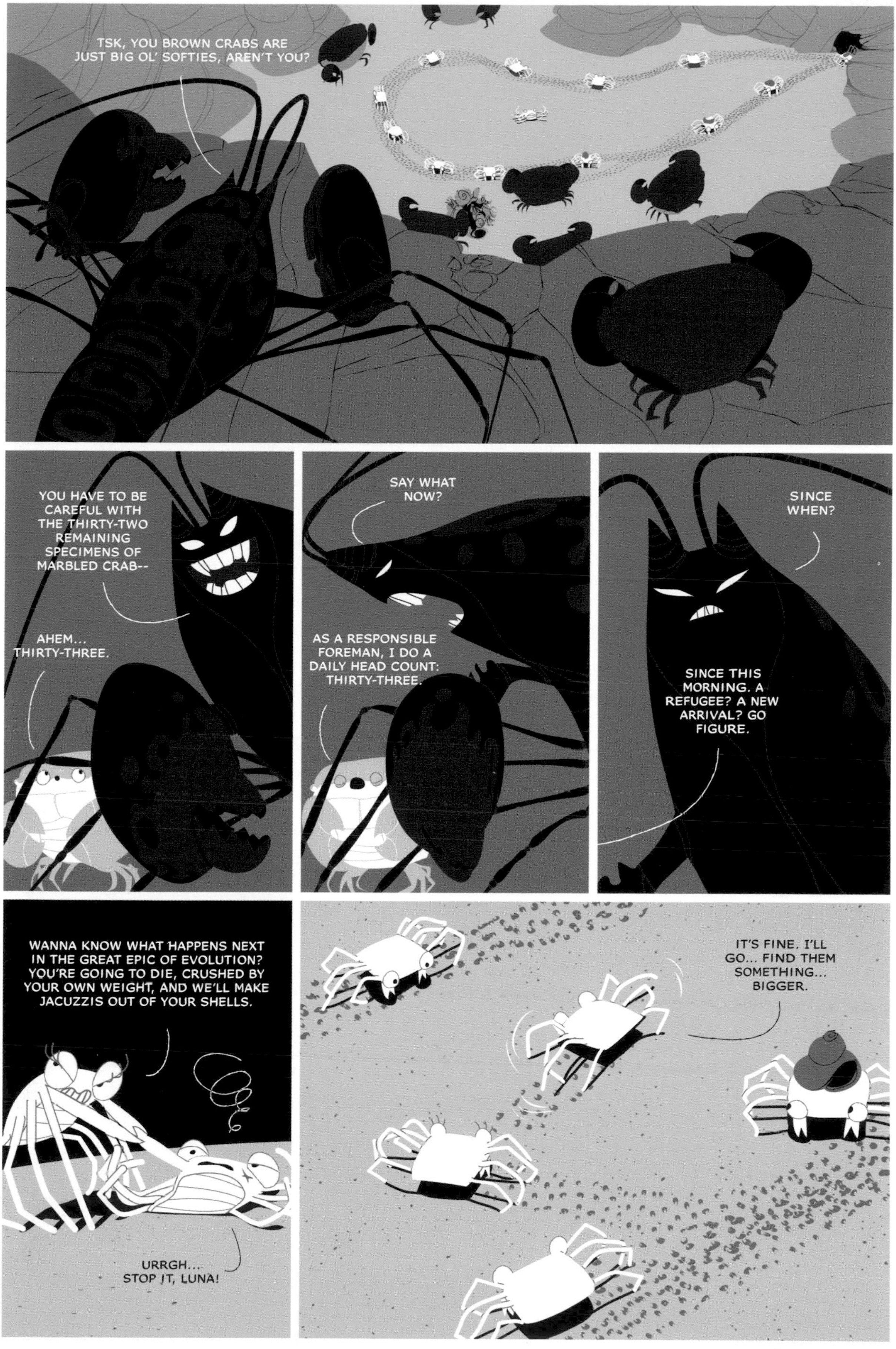
TSK, YOU BROWN CRABS ARE JUST BIG OL' SOFTIES, AREN'T YOU?
YOU HAVE TO BE CAREFUL WITH THE THIRTY-TWO REMAINING SPECIMENS OF MARBLED CRAB--
AHEM... THIRTY-THREE.
SAY WHAT NOW?
AS A RESPONSIBLE FOREMAN, I DO A DAILY HEAD COUNT: THIRTY-THREE.
SINCE WHEN?
SINCE THIS MORNING. A REFUGEE? A NEW ARRIVAL? GO FIGURE.
WANNA KNOW WHAT HAPPENS NEXT IN THE GREAT EPIC OF EVOLUTION? YOU'RE GOING TO DIE, CRUSHED BY YOUR OWN WEIGHT, AND WE'LL MAKE JACUZZIS OUT OF YOUR SHELLS.
URRGH... STOP IT, LUNA!
IT'S FINE. I'LL GO... FIND THEM SOMETHING... BIGGER.

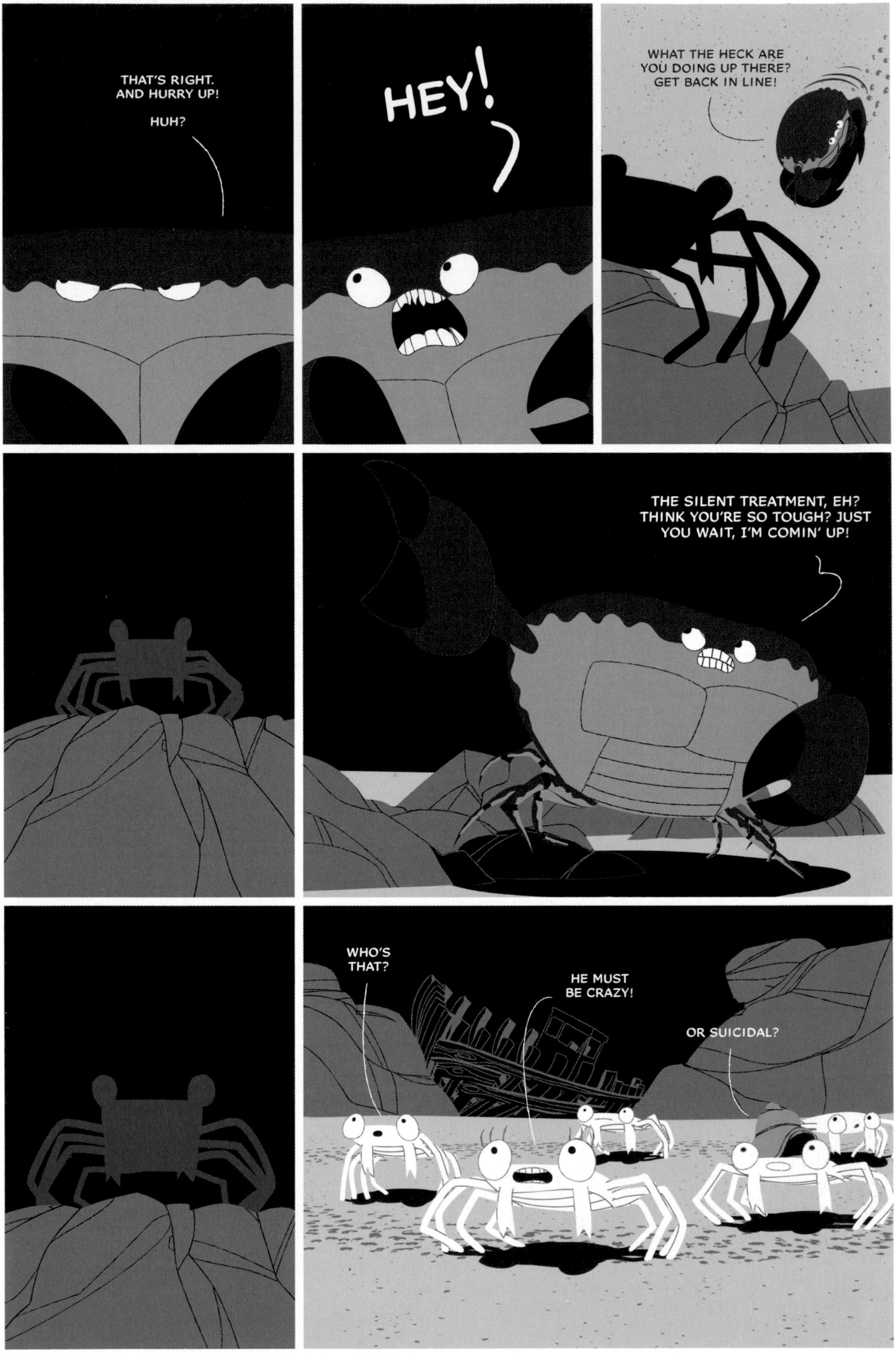
THAT'S RIGHT.
AND HURRY UP!
HUH?
HEY!
WHAT THE HECK ARE YOU DOING UP THERE? GET BACK IN LINE!
THE SILENT TREATMENT, EH? THINK YOU'RE SO TOUGH? JUST YOU WAIT, I'M COMIN' UP!
WHO'S THAT?
HE MUST BE CRAZY!
OR SUICIDAL?

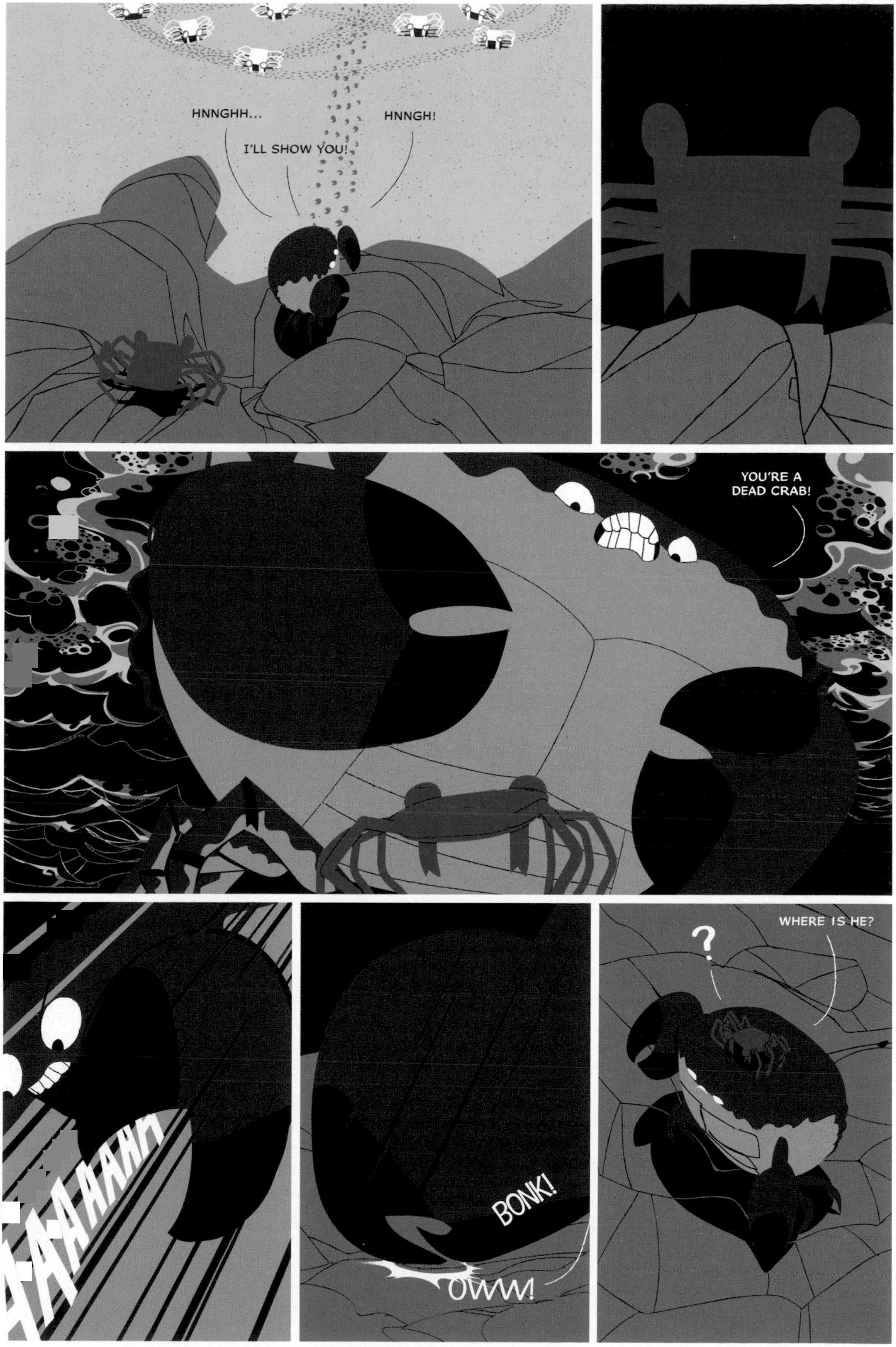
HNNGHH...
I'LL SHOW YOU!
HNNGH!
YOU'RE A DEAD CRAB!
BONK!
OWW!
?
WHERE IS HE?

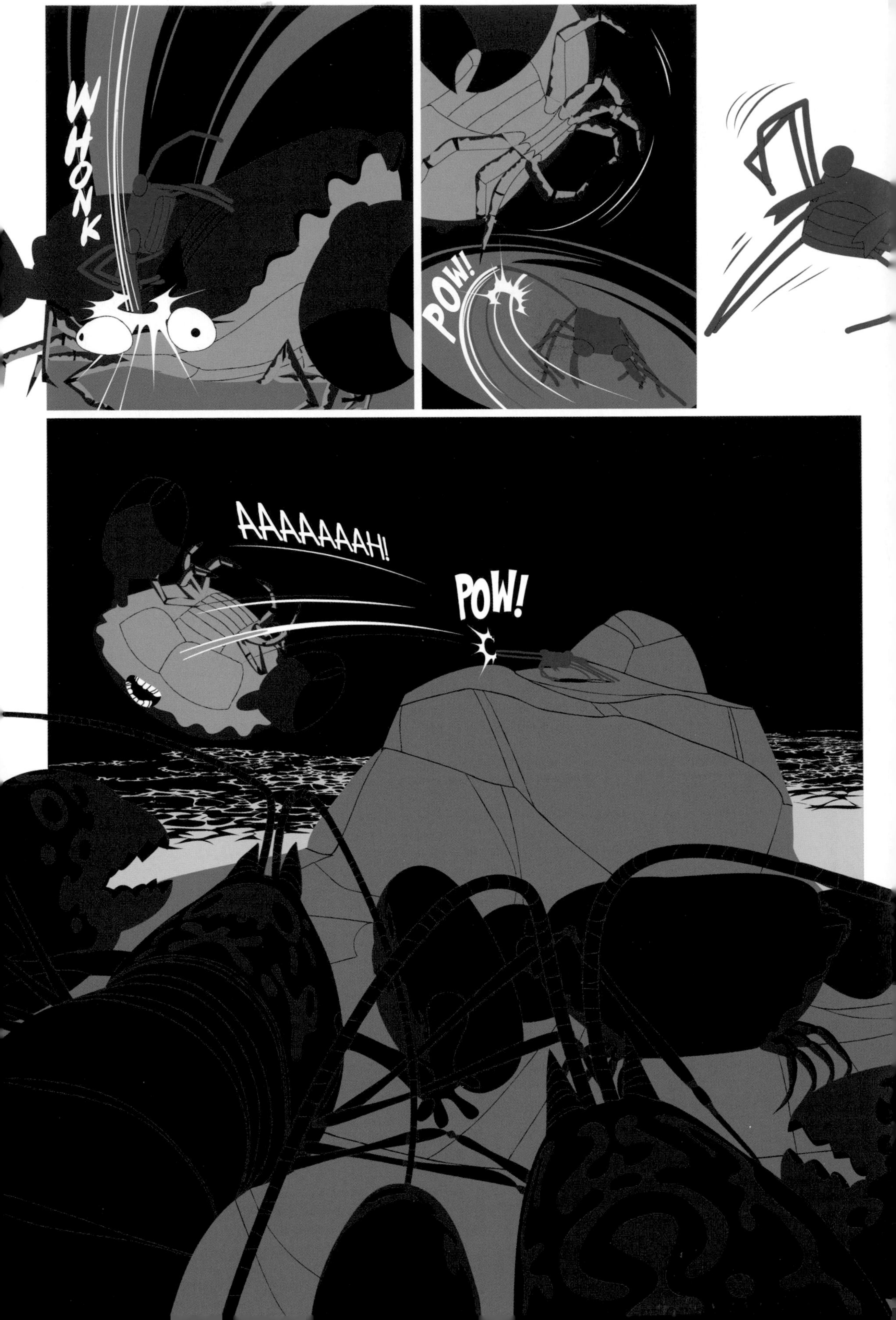
WHONK
POW!
AAAAAAAH!
POW!

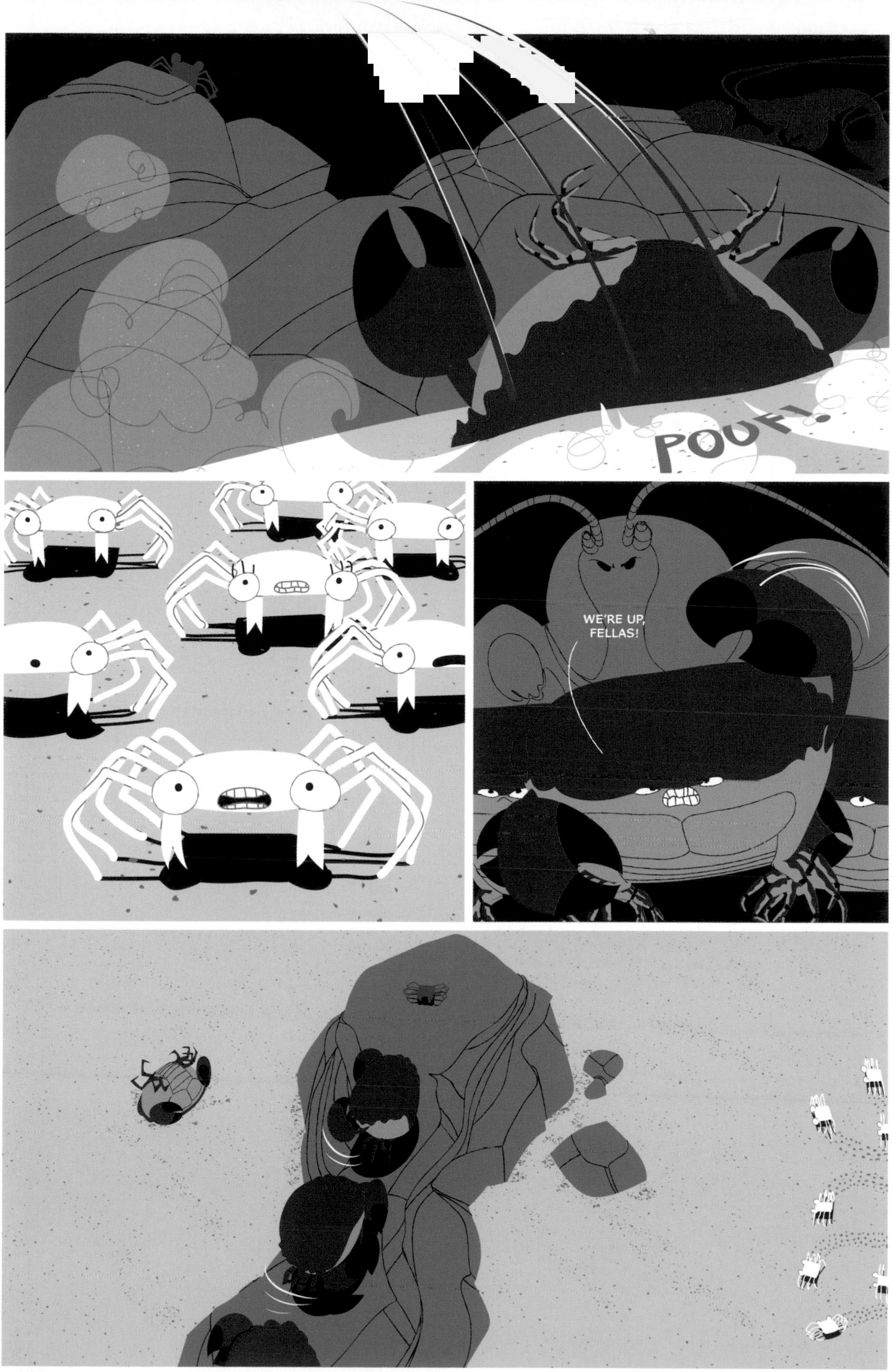
POUF!
WE'RE UP, FELLAS!

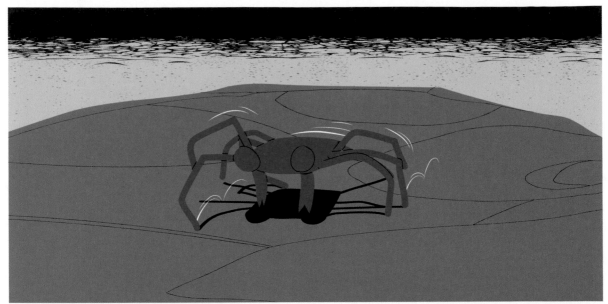

HEY! HE'S COMIN' RIGHT AT US!

THAT'S CRABTISTICALLY IMPOSSIBLE!

NOT JUST WALKING... I CAN RUN, TOO!

WHAT'S GOING ON UP THERE, GUYS?

PAF! PIF! PAF!

BING

POUF!

POUF!

SUNNY!

SUNNY!

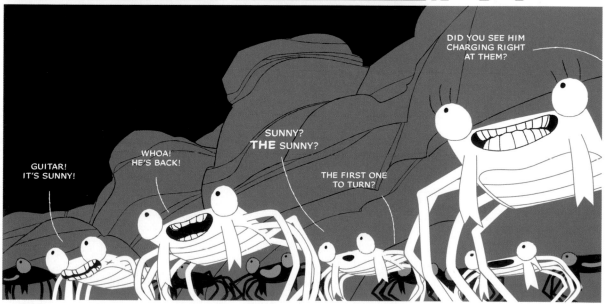

DID YOU SEE HIM CHARGING RIGHT AT THEM?

SUNNY? **THE** SUNNY?

THE FIRST ONE TO TURN?

WHOA! HE'S BACK!

GUITAR! IT'S SUNNY!

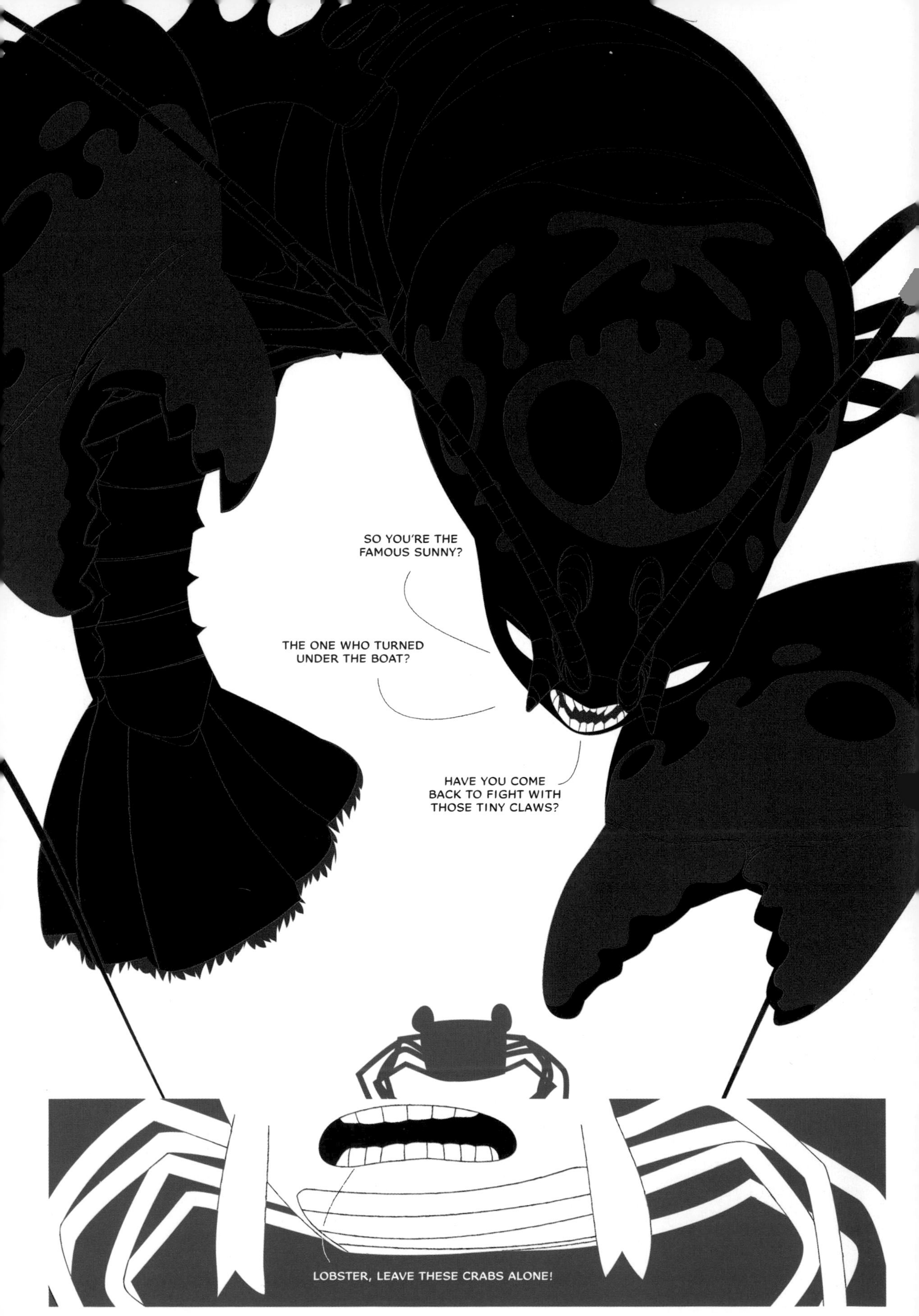
SO YOU'RE THE FAMOUS SUNNY?
THE ONE WHO TURNED UNDER THE BOAT?
HAVE YOU COME BACK TO FIGHT WITH THOSE TINY CLAWS?
LOBSTER, LEAVE THESE CRABS ALONE!

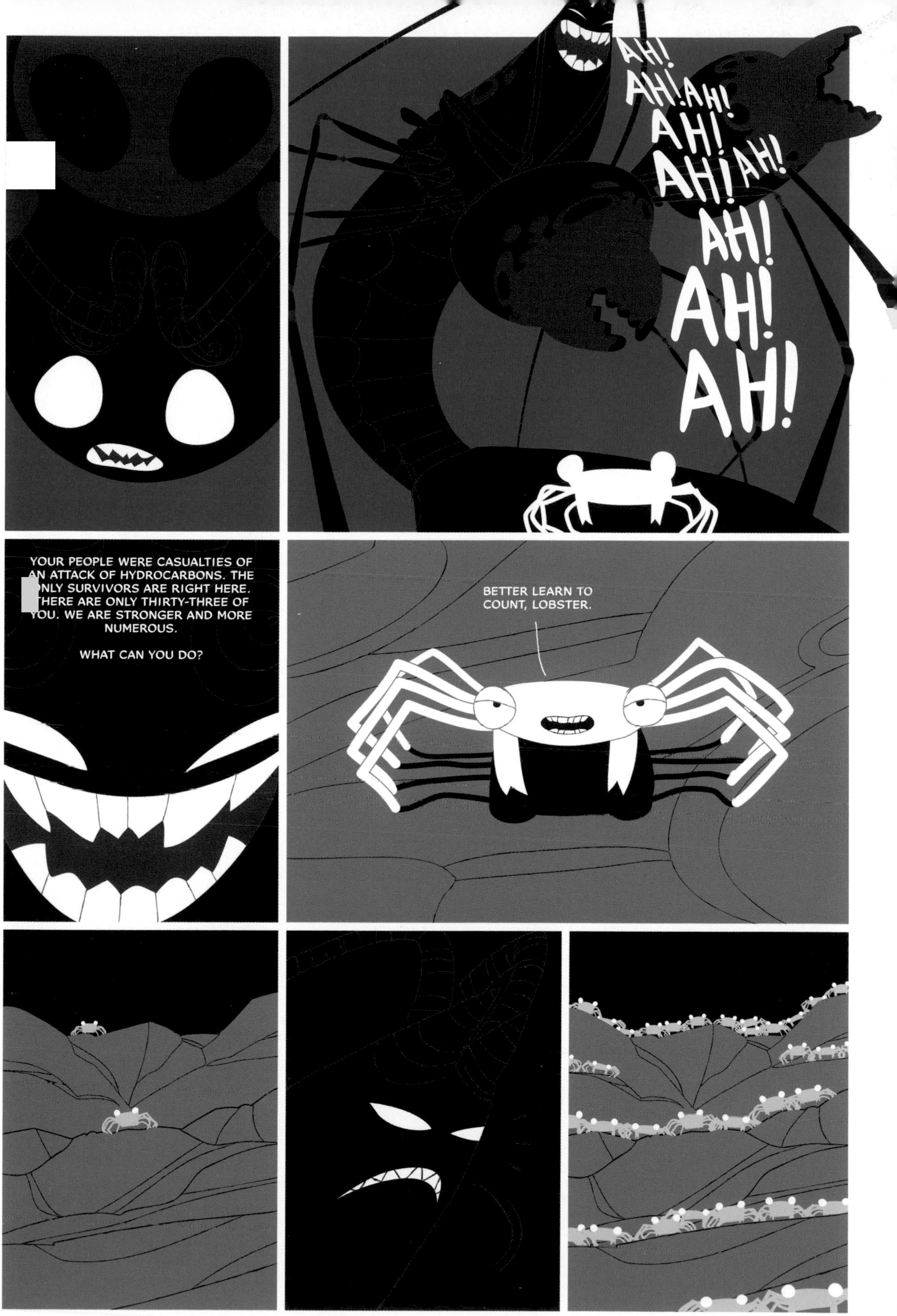
AH! AH! AH! AH! AH! AH! AH! AH! AH! AH!
YOUR PEOPLE WERE CASUALTIES OF AN ATTACK OF HYDROCARBONS. THE ONLY SURVIVORS ARE RIGHT HERE. THERE ARE ONLY THIRTY-THREE OF YOU. WE ARE STRONGER AND MORE NUMEROUS.
WHAT CAN YOU DO?
BETTER LEARN TO COUNT, LOBSTER.

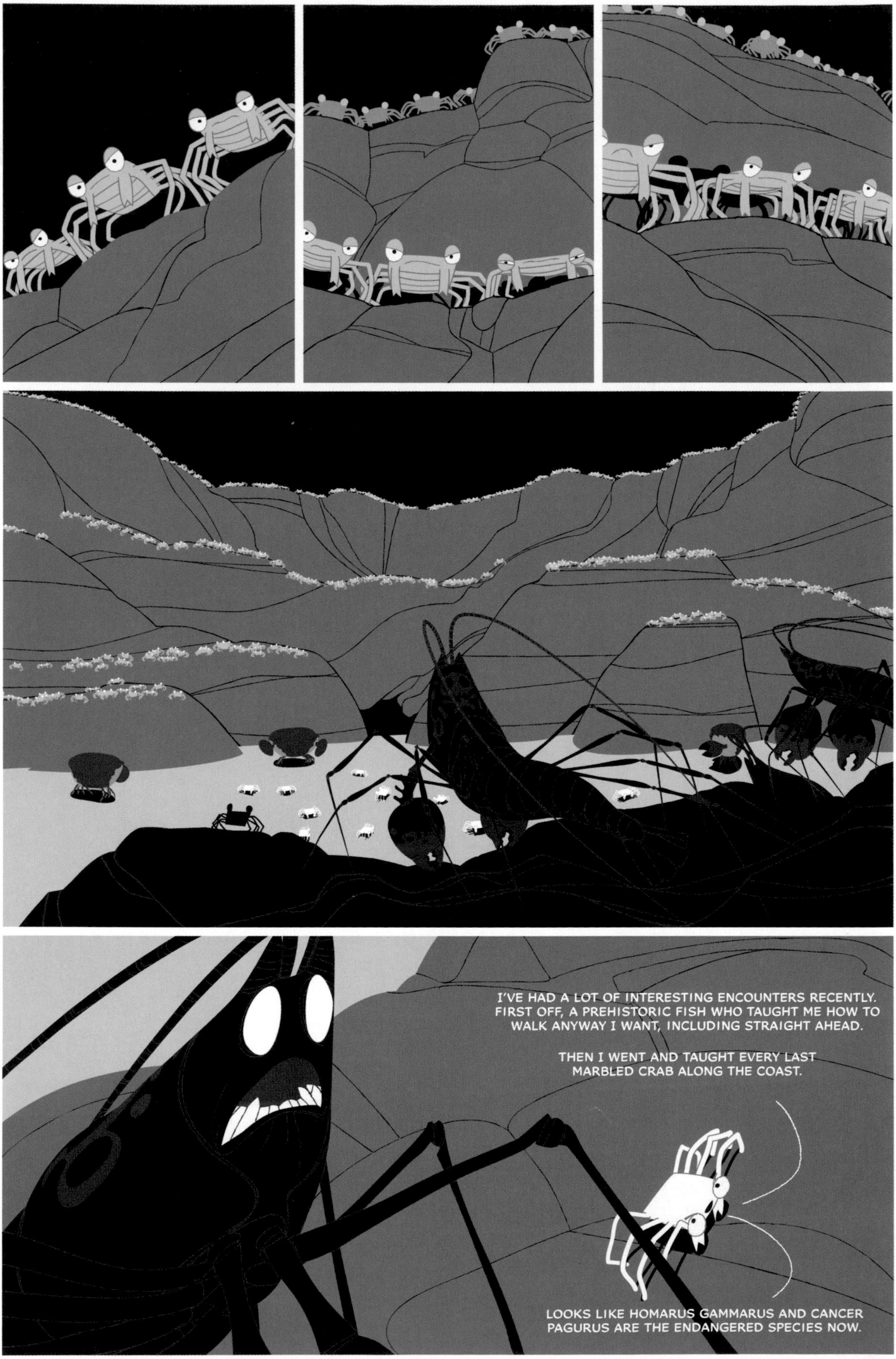
I'VE HAD A LOT OF INTERESTING ENCOUNTERS RECENTLY. FIRST OFF, A PREHISTORIC FISH WHO TAUGHT ME HOW TO WALK ANYWAY I WANT, INCLUDING STRAIGHT AHEAD.
THEN I WENT AND TAUGHT EVERY LAST MARBLED CRAB ALONG THE COAST.
LOOKS LIKE HOMARUS GAMMARUS AND CANCER PAGURUS ARE THE ENDANGERED SPECIES NOW.

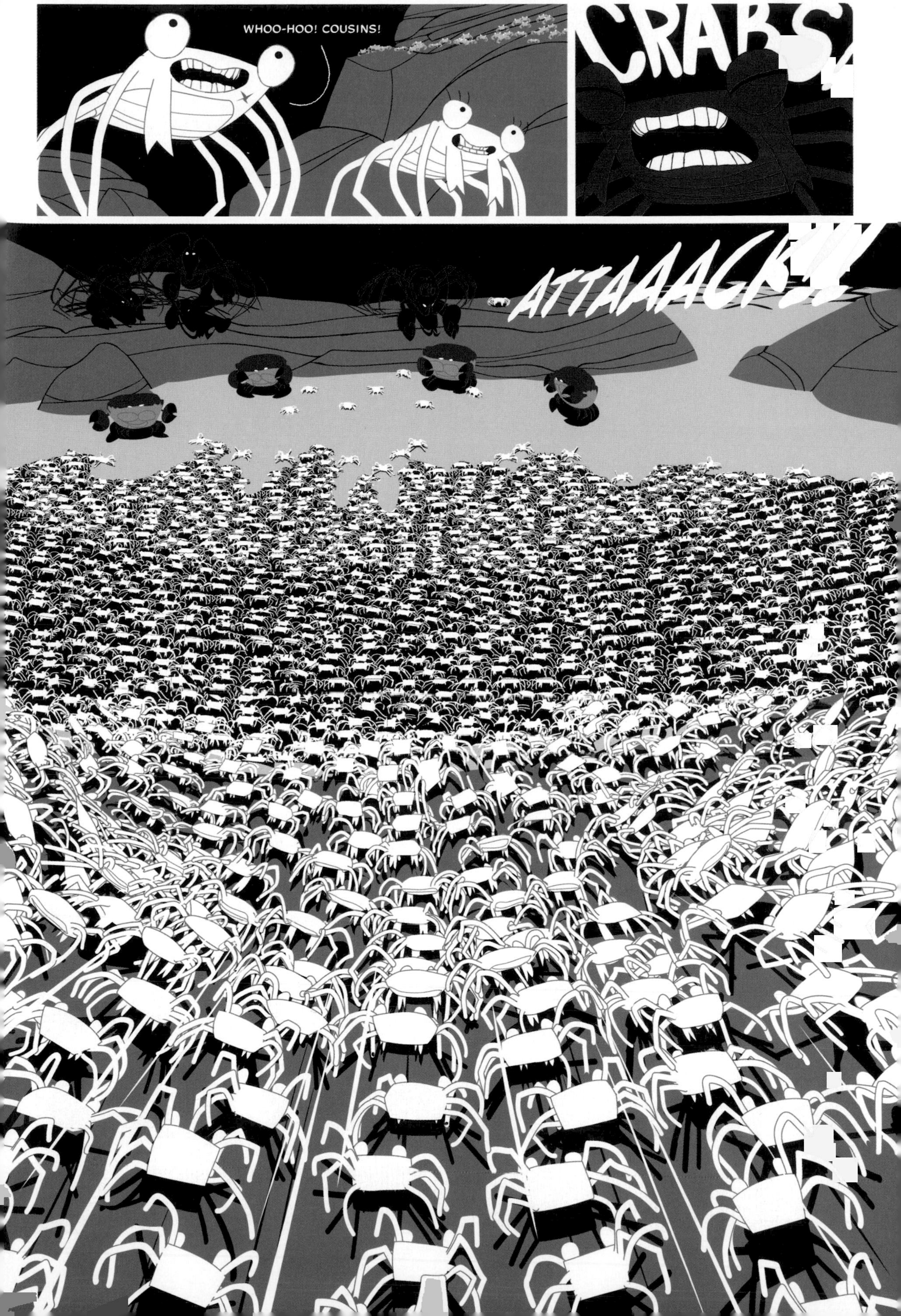
WHOO-HOO! COUSINS!
CRABS
ATTAAAACK

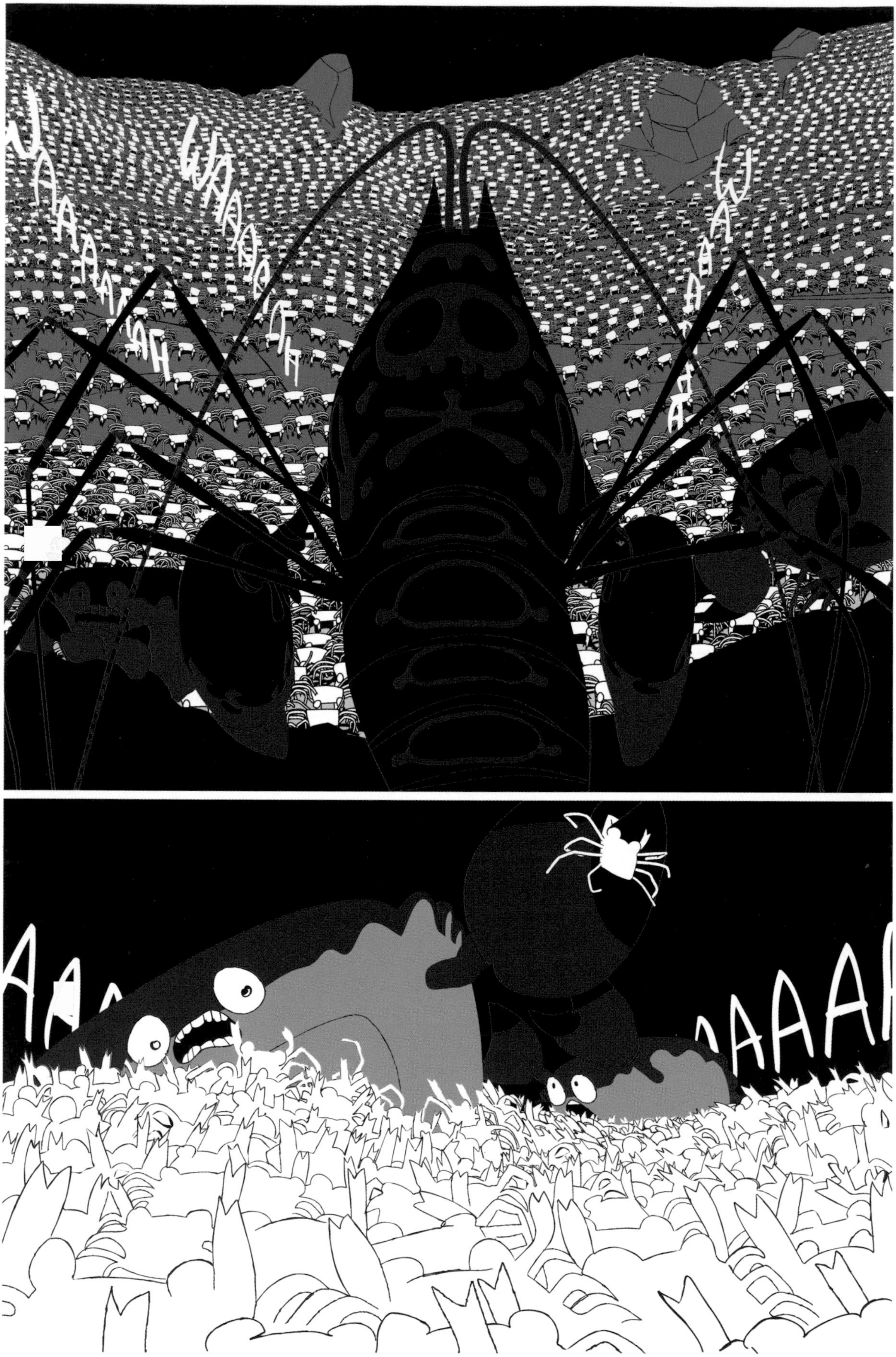
AAAAA

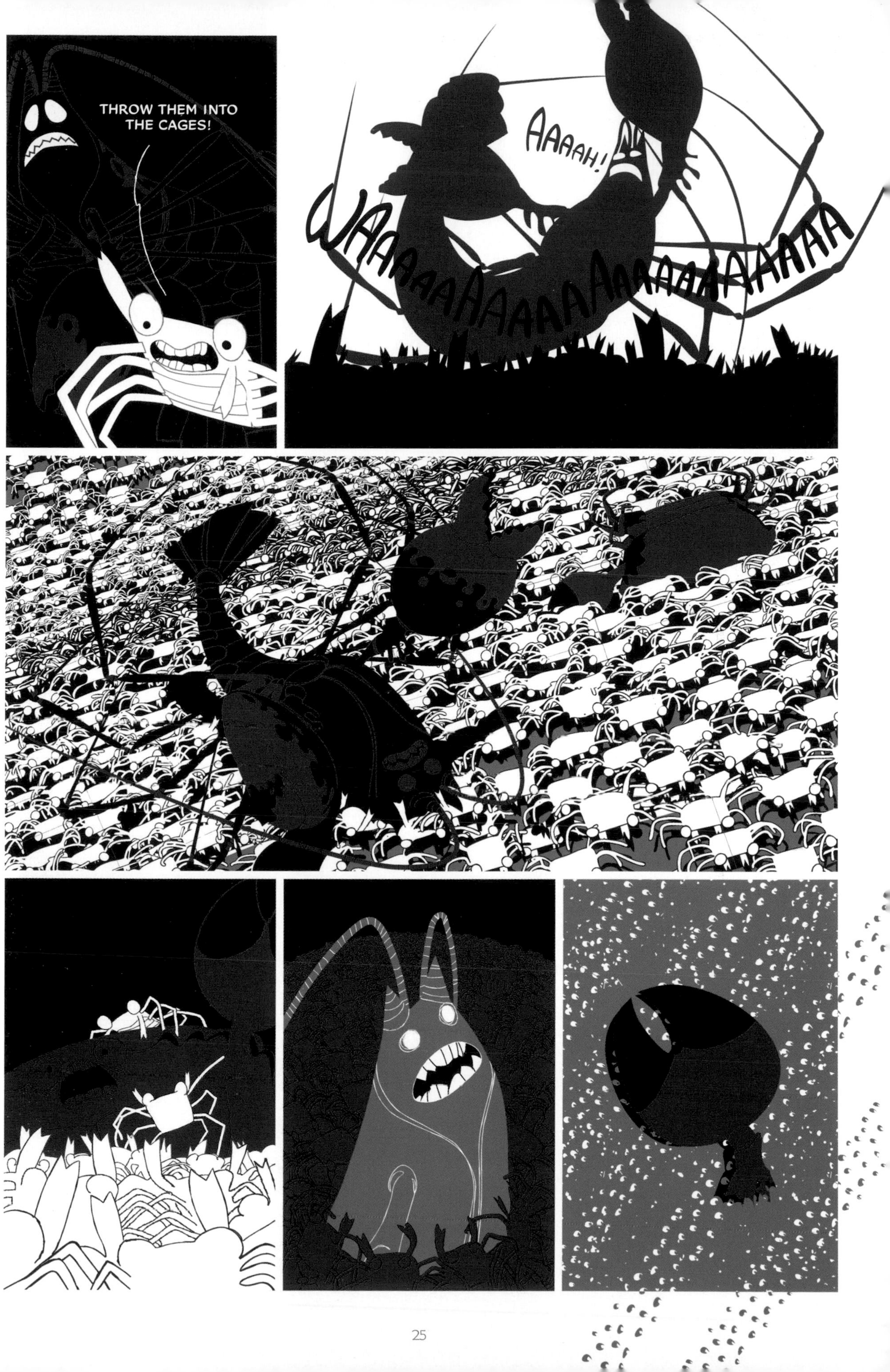
THROW THEM INTO THE CAGES!
AAAAH!
WAAAAAAAAAAAAAAAAAAAAAAA

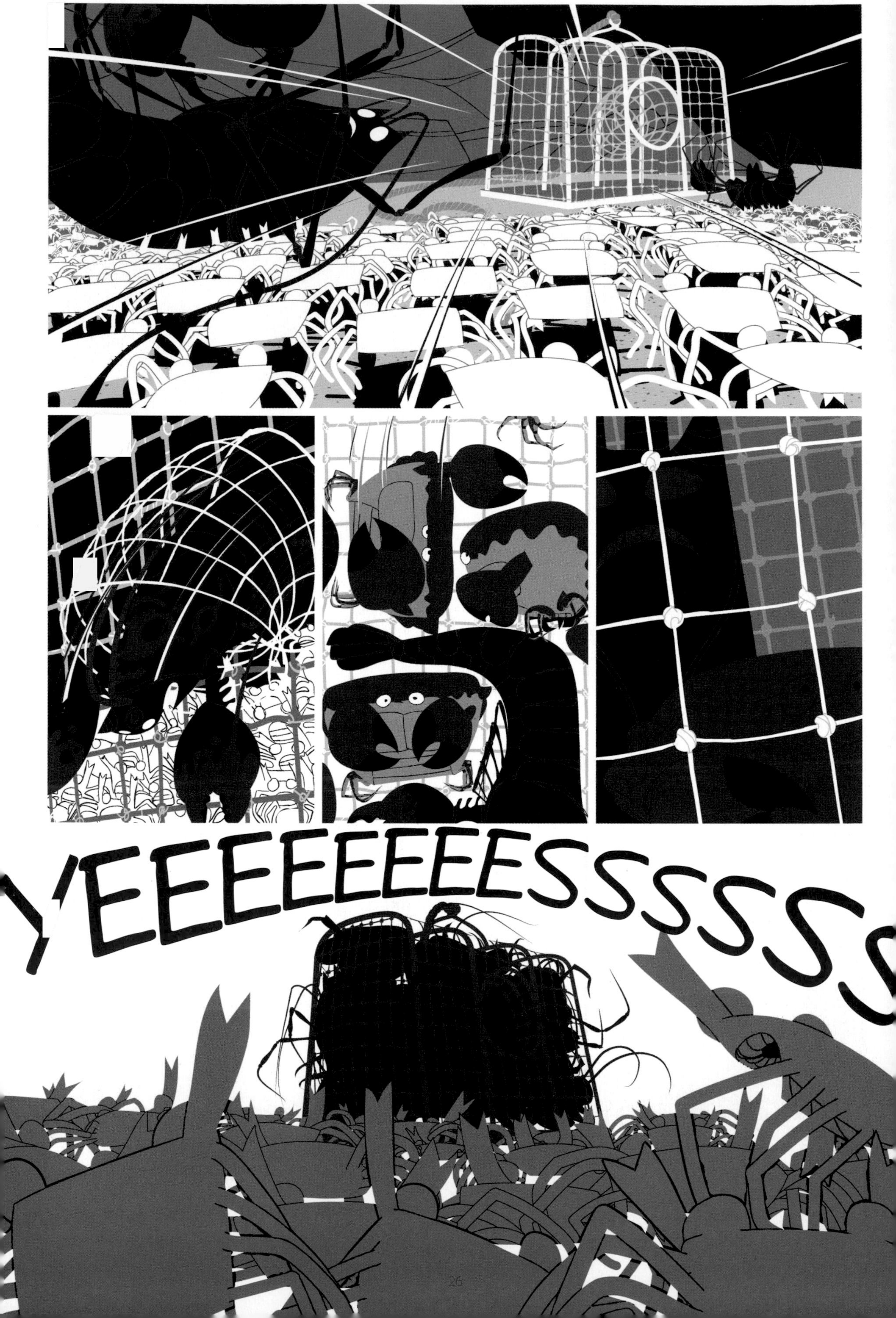
YEEEEEEEESSSSSS

SUNNY!

SUNNY! SUNNY! SUNNY! SUNNY! SUNNY! SUNNY!

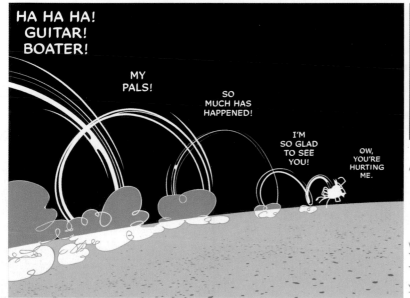

HA HA HA! GUITAR! BOATER!

MY PALS!

SO MUCH HAS HAPPENED!

I'M SO GLAD TO SEE YOU!

OW, YOU'RE HURTING ME.

SUNNY! YOU MUST ADDRESS YOUR PEOPLE!

MY WHAT NOW?

MAKE A SPEECH OR SOMETHING--I DUNNO!

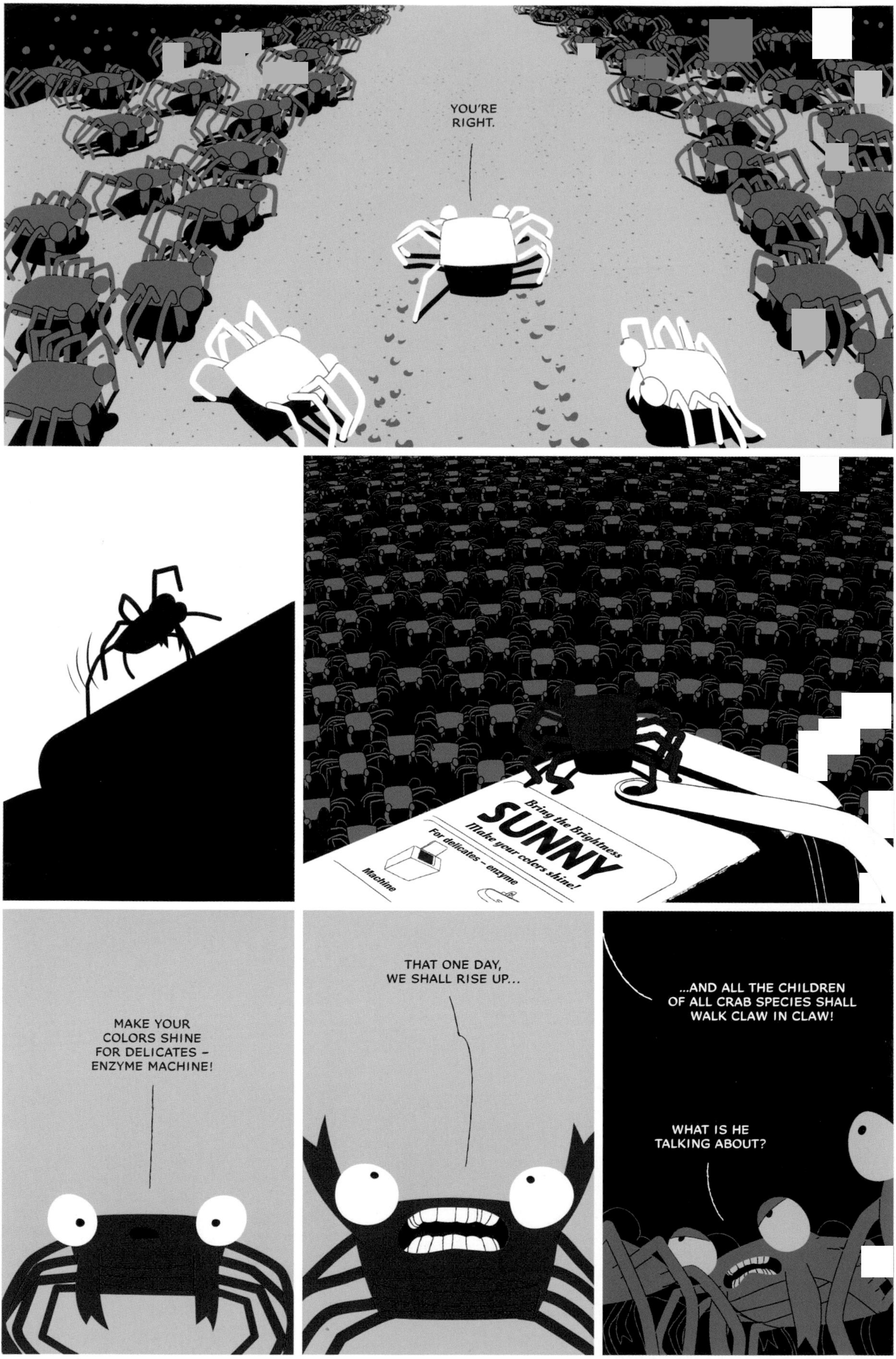
YOU'RE RIGHT.
Bring the Brightness
SUNNY
Make your colors shine!
For delicates – enzyme
Machine
MAKE YOUR COLORS SHINE FOR DELICATES – ENZYME MACHINE!
THAT ONE DAY, WE SHALL RISE UP...
...AND ALL THE CHILDREN OF ALL CRAB SPECIES SHALL WALK CLAW IN CLAW!
WHAT IS HE TALKING ABOUT?

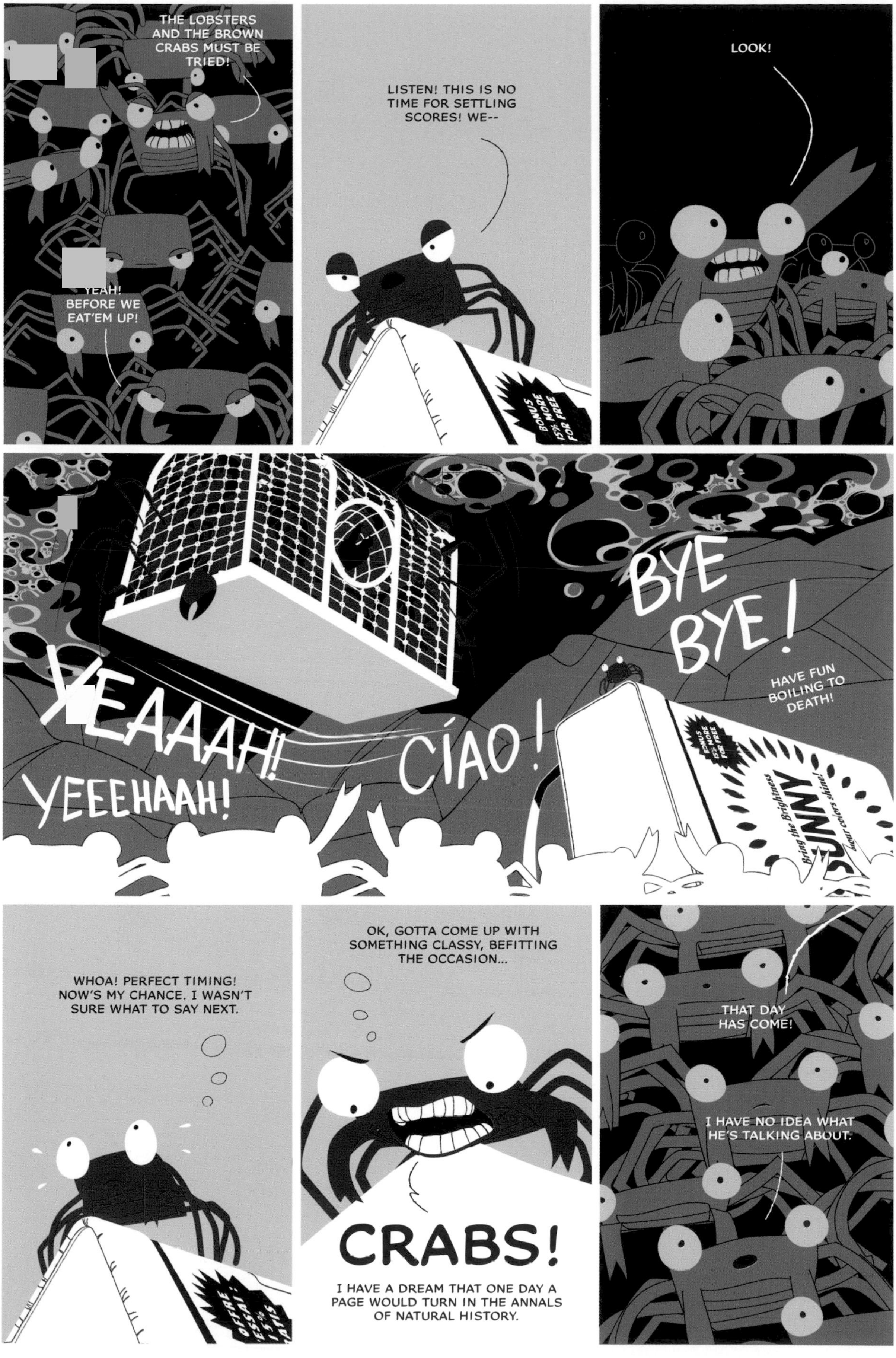
THE LOBSTERS AND THE BROWN CRABS MUST BE TRIED!
YEAH! BEFORE WE EAT'EM UP!
LISTEN! THIS IS NO TIME FOR SETTLING SCORES! WE--
BONUS 15% MORE FOR FREE
LOOK!
YEAAAH!
YEEEHAAH!
CIAO!
BYE BYE!
HAVE FUN BOILING TO DEATH!
BONUS 15% MORE FOR FREE
WHOA! PERFECT TIMING! NOW'S MY CHANCE. I WASN'T SURE WHAT TO SAY NEXT.
OK, GOTTA COME UP WITH SOMETHING CLASSY, BEFITTING THE OCCASION...
CRABS!
I HAVE A DREAM THAT ONE DAY A PAGE WOULD TURN IN THE ANNALS OF NATURAL HISTORY.
THAT DAY HAS COME!
I HAVE NO IDEA WHAT HE'S TALKING ABOUT.

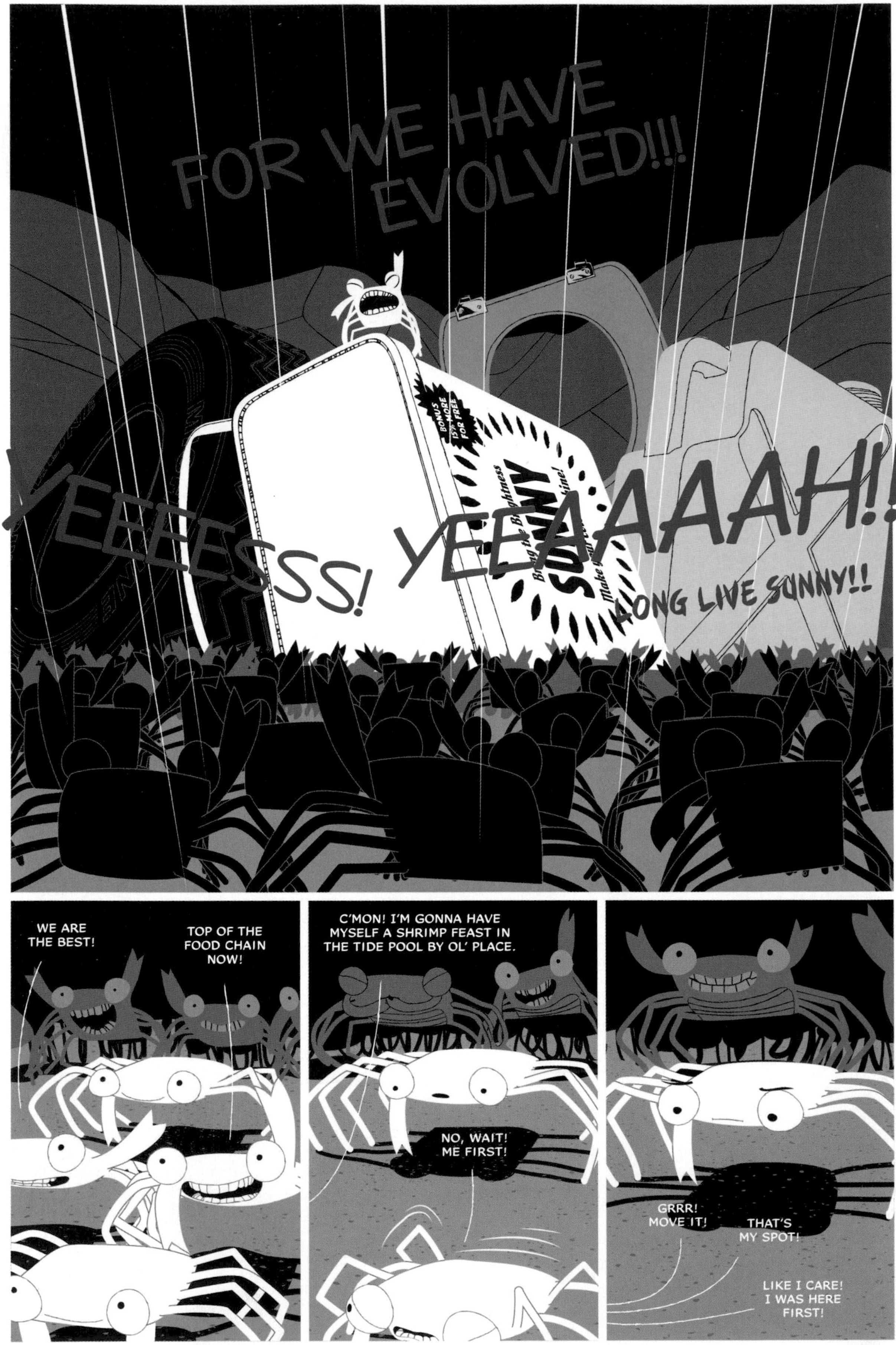
FOR WE HAVE EVOLVED!!!
BONUS
SUNNY
Bring the Brightness
YEEEESSS!
YEEAAAAH!!
LONG LIVE SUNNY!!
WE ARE THE BEST!
TOP OF THE FOOD CHAIN NOW!
C'MON! I'M GONNA HAVE MYSELF A SHRIMP FEAST IN THE TIDE POOL BY OL' PLACE.
NO, WAIT! ME FIRST!
GRRR! MOVE IT!
THAT'S MY SPOT!
LIKE I CARE! I WAS HERE FIRST!

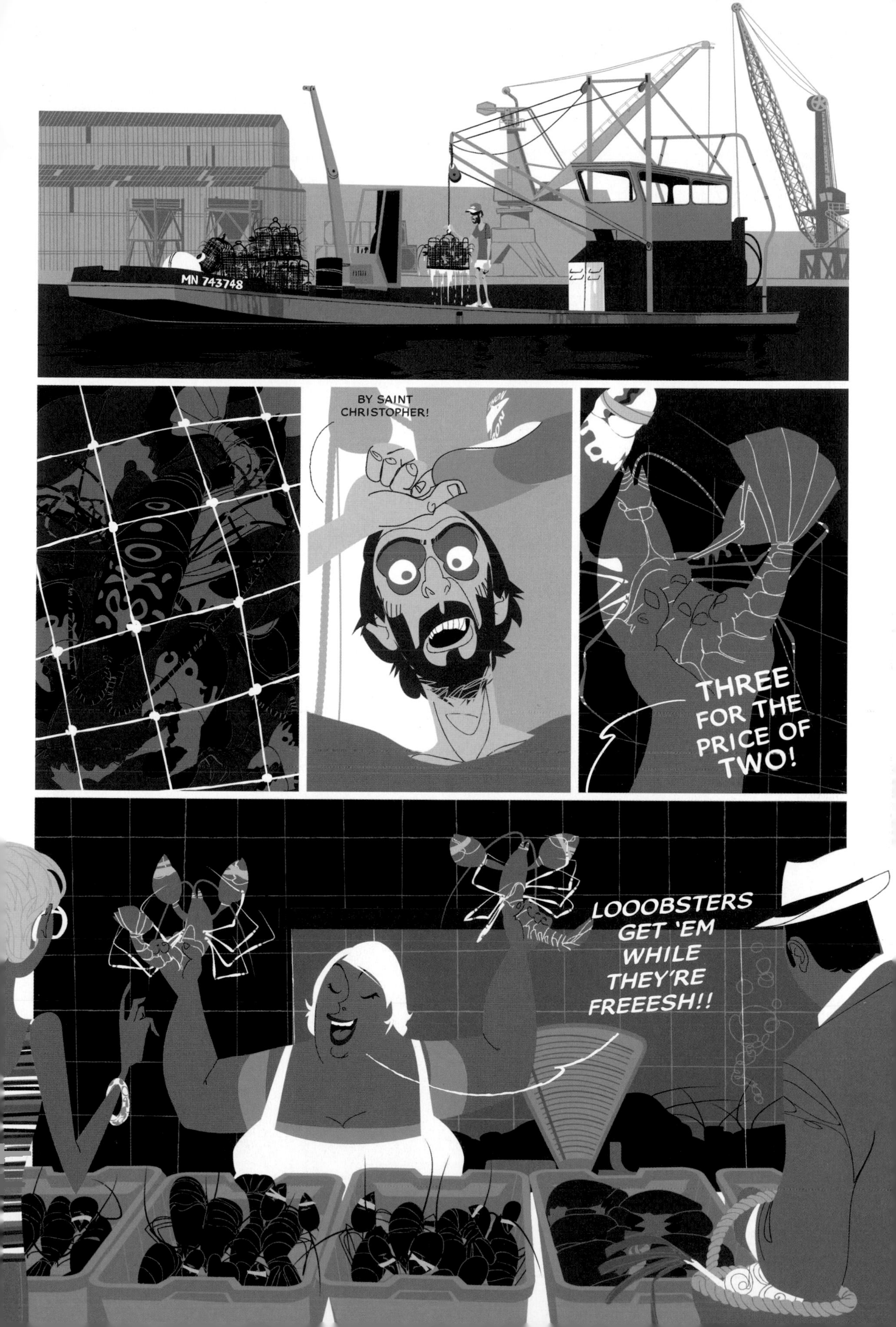
MN 743748
BY SAINT CHRISTOPHER!
THREE FOR THE PRICE OF TWO!
LOOOBSTERS GET 'EM WHILE THEY'RE FREEESH!!

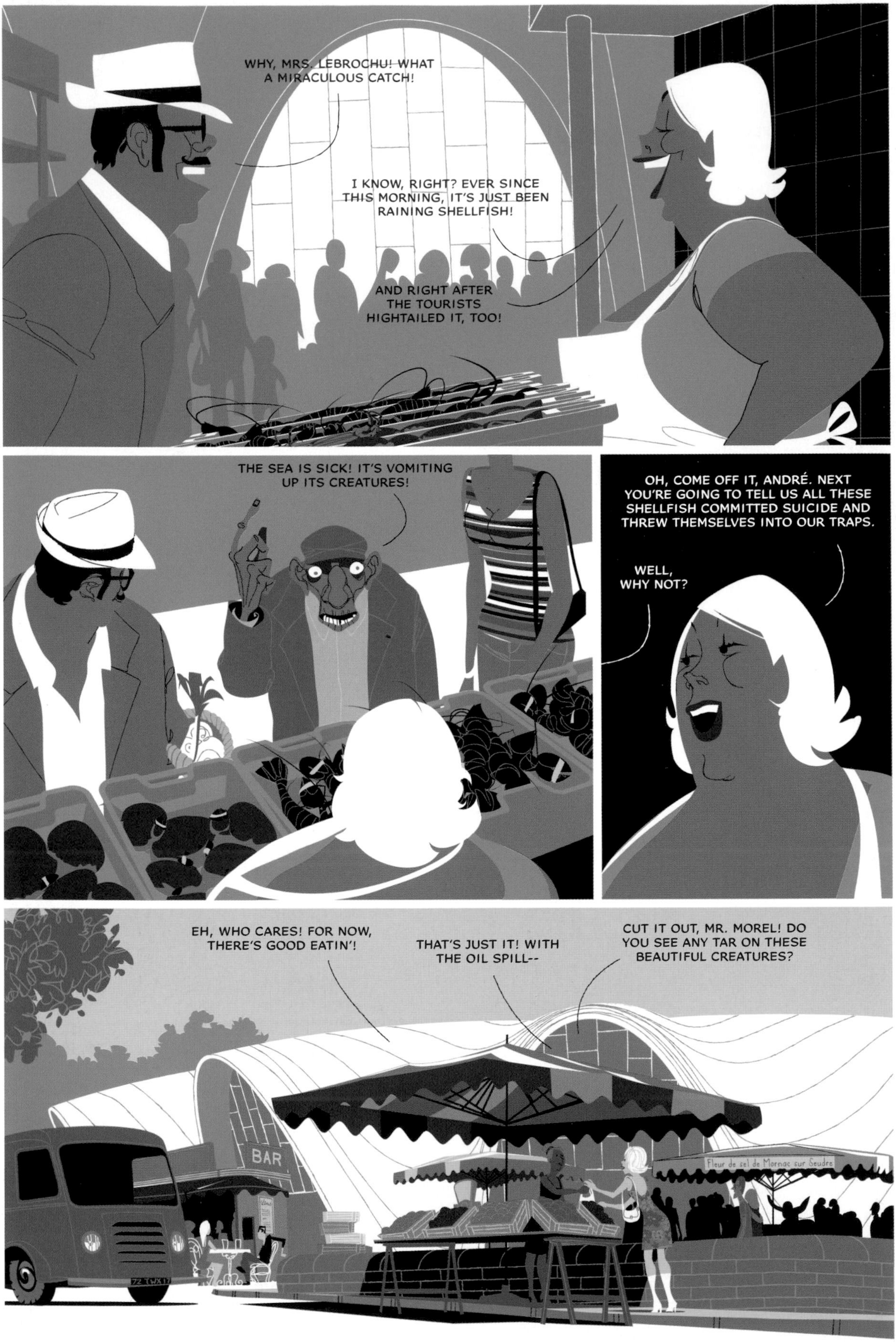
WHY, MRS. LEBROCHU! WHAT A MIRACULOUS CATCH!
I KNOW, RIGHT? EVER SINCE THIS MORNING, IT'S JUST BEEN RAINING SHELLFISH!
AND RIGHT AFTER THE TOURISTS HIGHTAILED IT, TOO!
THE SEA IS SICK! IT'S VOMITING UP ITS CREATURES!
OH, COME OFF IT, ANDRÉ. NEXT YOU'RE GOING TO TELL US ALL THESE SHELLFISH COMMITTED SUICIDE AND THREW THEMSELVES INTO OUR TRAPS.
WELL, WHY NOT?
EH, WHO CARES! FOR NOW, THERE'S GOOD EATIN'!
THAT'S JUST IT! WITH THE OIL SPILL--
CUT IT OUT, MR. MOREL! DO YOU SEE ANY TAR ON THESE BEAUTIFUL CREATURES?
BAR
Fleur de sel de Mornac sur Seudre

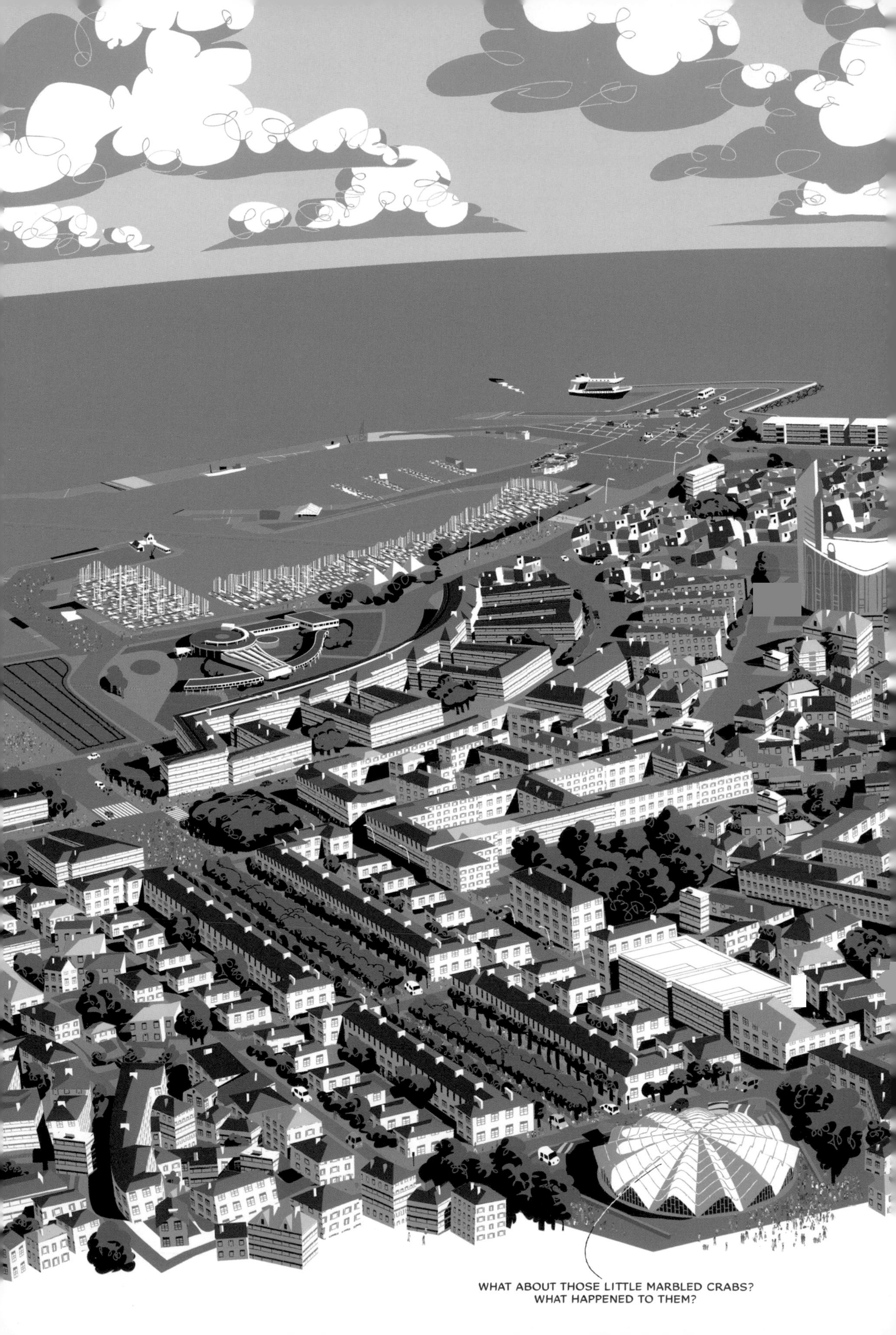
WHAT ABOUT THOSE LITTLE MARBLED CRABS?
WHAT HAPPENED TO THEM?

ONE YEAR LATER...

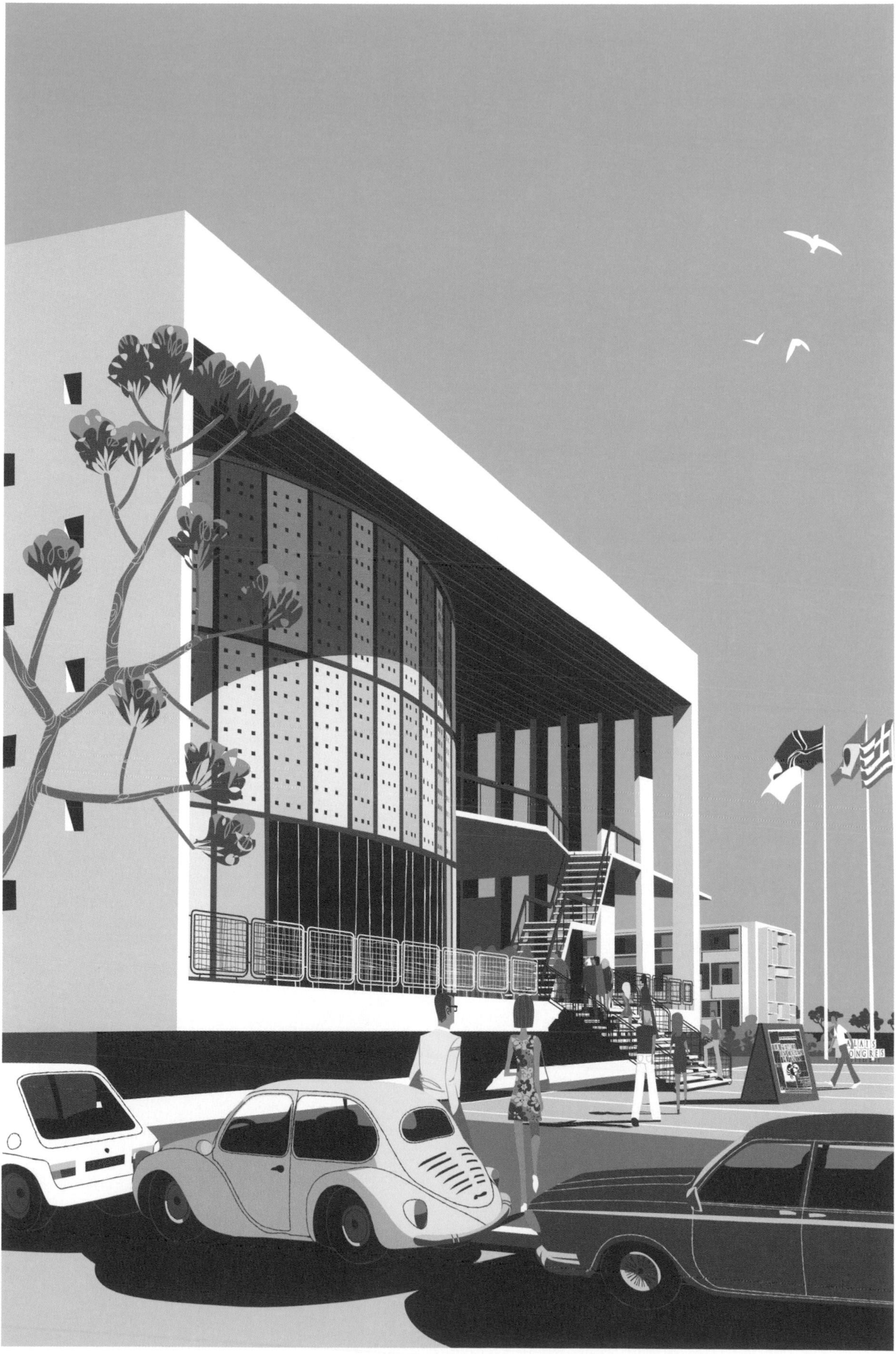
ALAIS
ONGRES

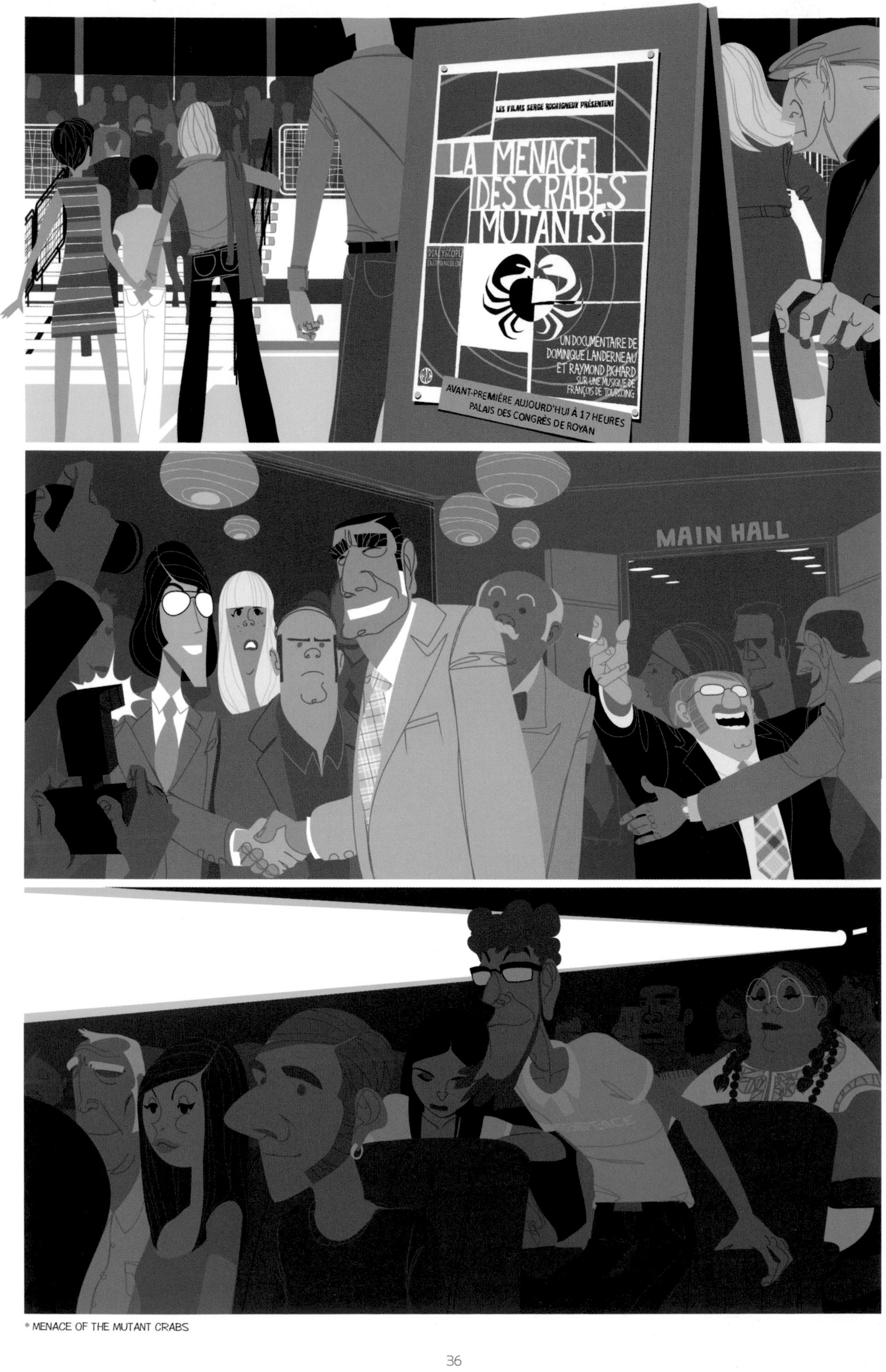
LES FILMS SERGE ROCHIGNEUX PRÉSENTENT
LA MENACE DES CRABES MUTANTS*
UN DOCUMENTAIRE DE DOMINIQUE LANDERNEAU ET RAYMOND PICHARD
SUR UNE MUSIQUE DE FRANÇOIS DE TOURCOING
AVANT-PREMIÈRE AUJOURD'HUI À 17 HEURES
PALAIS DES CONGRÈS DE ROYAN
MAIN HALL

* MENACE OF THE MUTANT CRABS

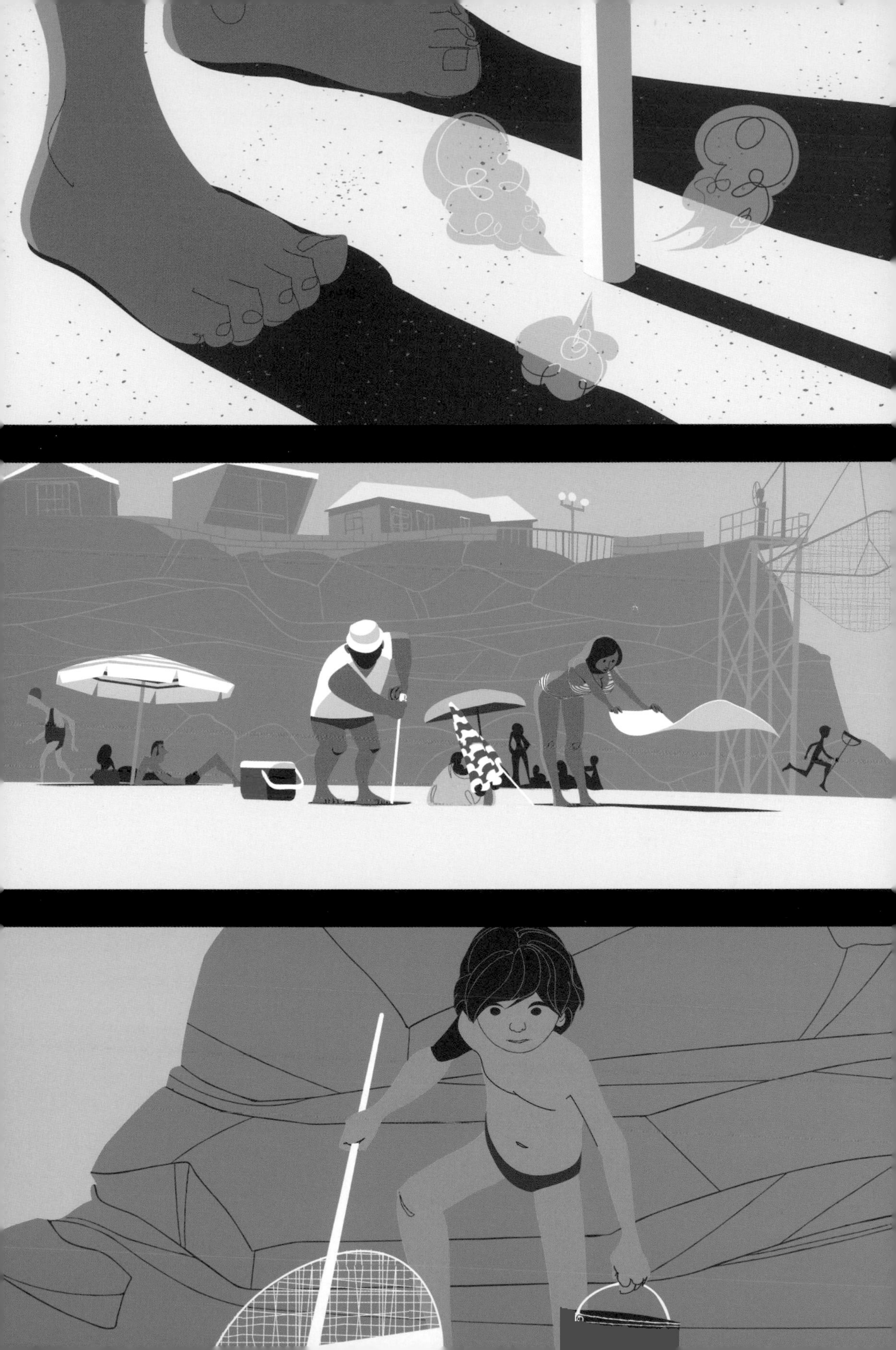

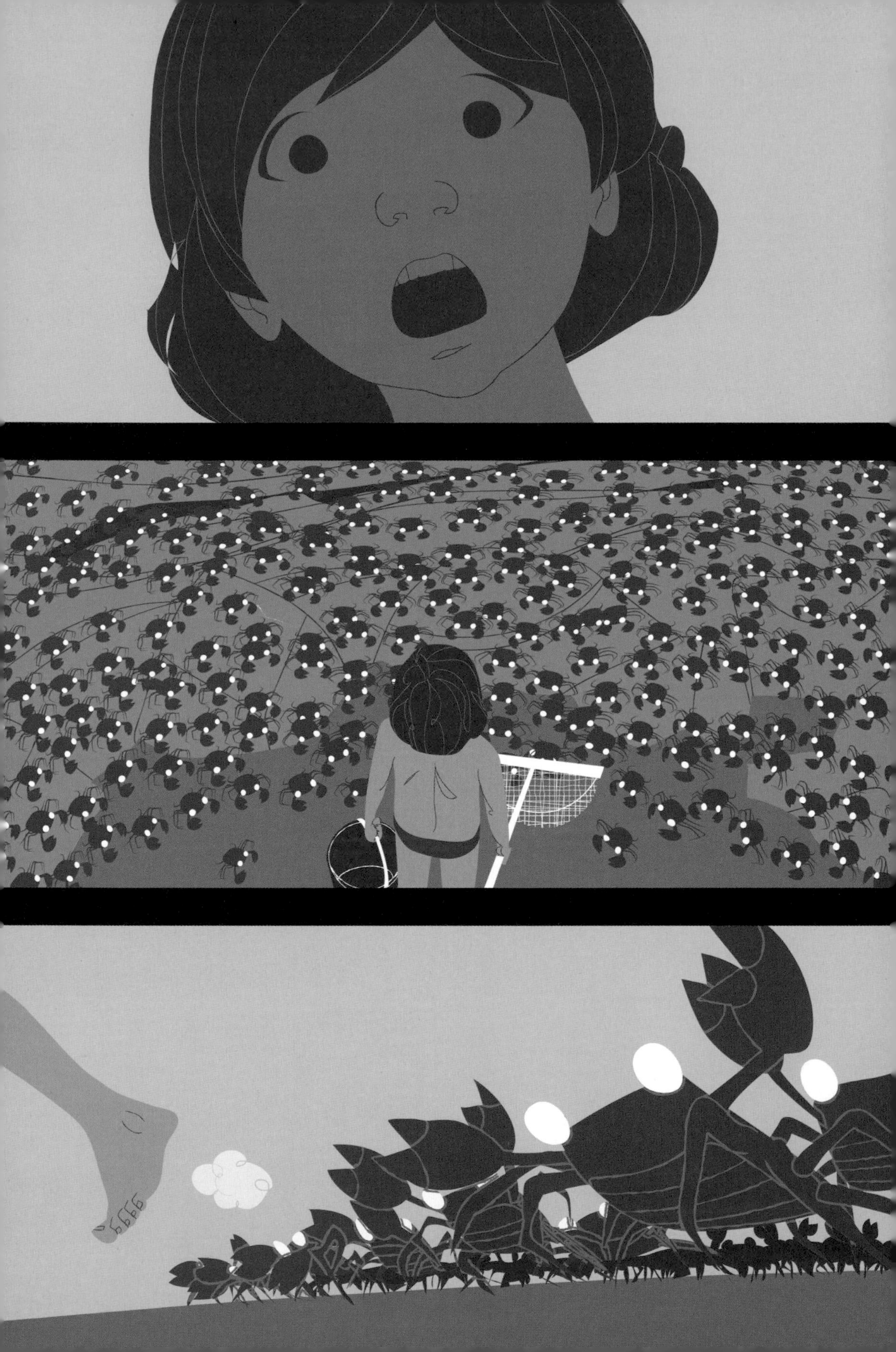

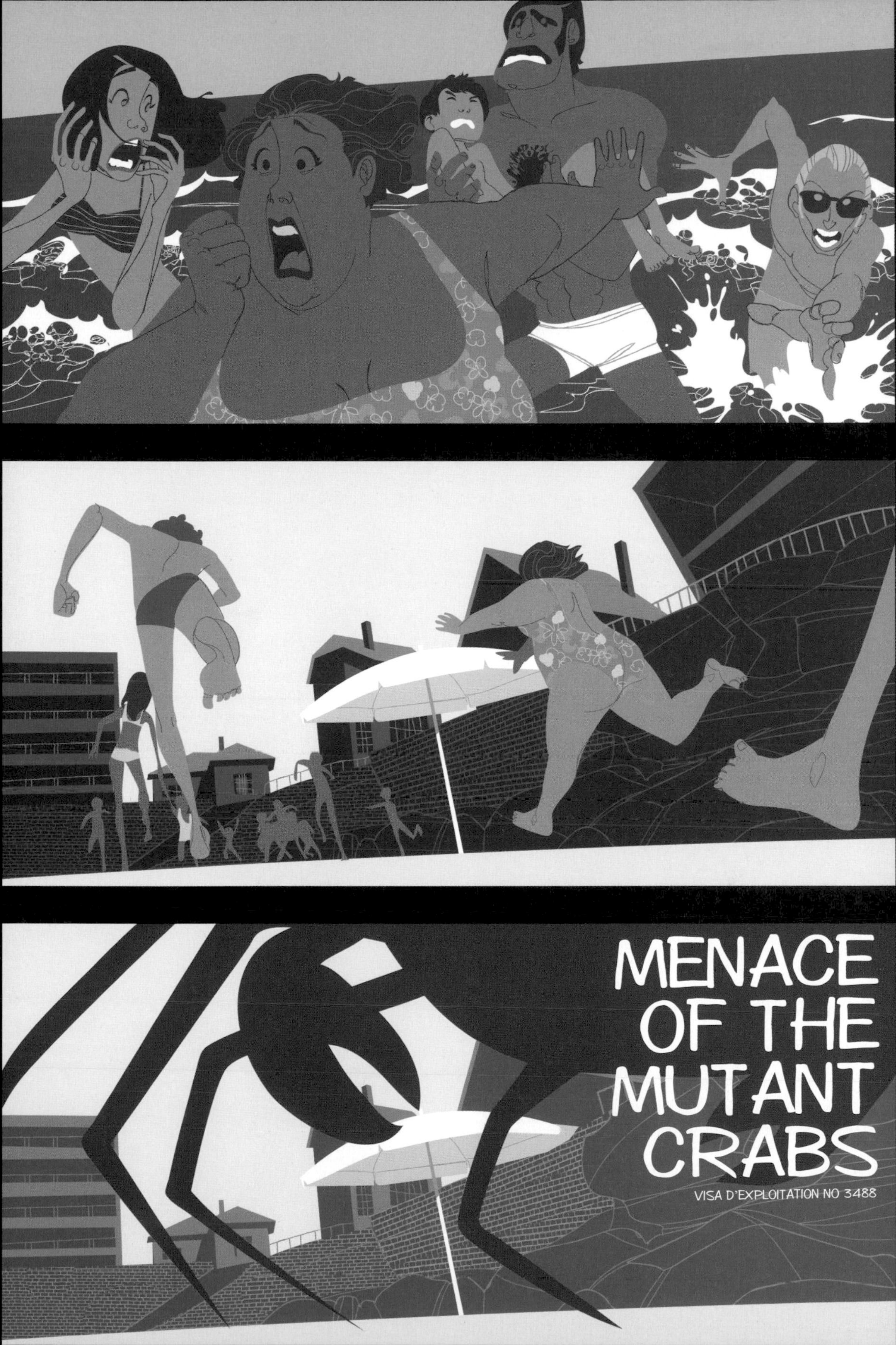
MENACE
OF THE
MUTANT
CRABS
VISA D'EXPLOITATION NO 3488

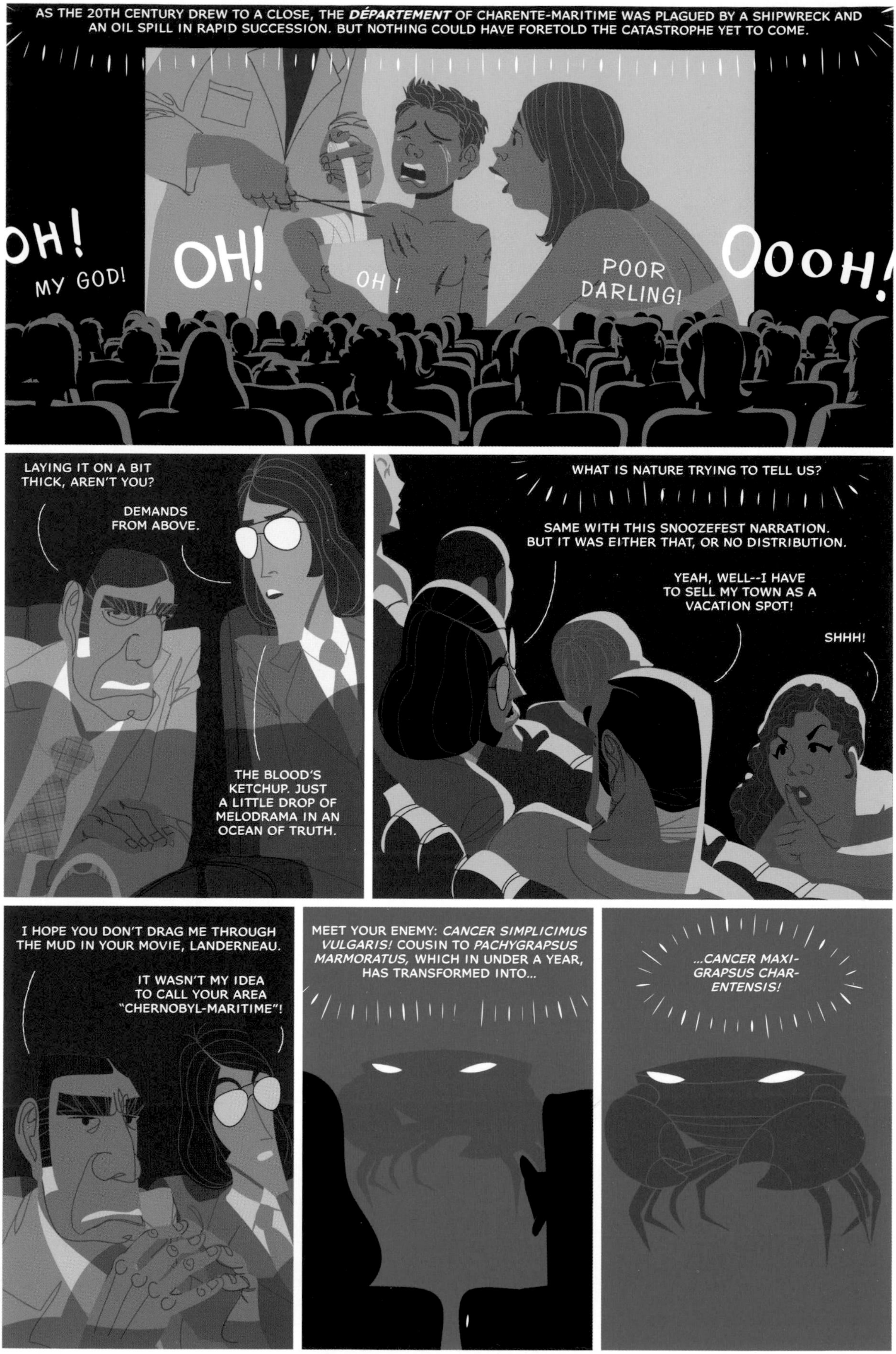
AS THE 20TH CENTURY DREW TO A CLOSE, THE *DÉPARTEMENT* OF CHARENTE-MARITIME WAS PLAGUED BY A SHIPWRECK AND AN OIL SPILL IN RAPID SUCCESSION. BUT NOTHING COULD HAVE FORETOLD THE CATASTROPHE YET TO COME.
OH!
MY GOD!
OH!
OH!
POOR DARLING!
OOOH!
LAYING IT ON A BIT THICK, AREN'T YOU?
DEMANDS FROM ABOVE.
THE BLOOD'S KETCHUP. JUST A LITTLE DROP OF MELODRAMA IN AN OCEAN OF TRUTH.
WHAT IS NATURE TRYING TO TELL US?
SAME WITH THIS SNOOZEFEST NARRATION. BUT IT WAS EITHER THAT, OR NO DISTRIBUTION.
YEAH, WELL--I HAVE TO SELL MY TOWN AS A VACATION SPOT!
SHHH!
I HOPE YOU DON'T DRAG ME THROUGH THE MUD IN YOUR MOVIE, LANDERNEAU.
IT WASN'T MY IDEA TO CALL YOUR AREA "CHERNOBYL-MARITIME"!
MEET YOUR ENEMY: *CANCER SIMPLICIMUS VULGARIS!* COUSIN TO *PACHYGRAPSUS MARMORATUS,* WHICH IN UNDER A YEAR, HAS TRANSFORMED INTO...
...CANCER MAXI-GRAPSUS CHAR-ENTENSIS!

THE MOST DREADED OF ALL UNDERSEA PREDATORS!

AAAAAAAH!!

PACK IT ALL UP. THE VACATIONERS HAVE GONE.

MOTHER NATURE IS TAKING HER REVENGE! MWAHAHAHA!

HEY! THAT'S ME!

WATCH OUT! THOSE CRABS COULD BUILD THEIR OWN PIPELINE SOMEDAY!

HAHAH!

HIHI

HA HA!

HAHAHA!

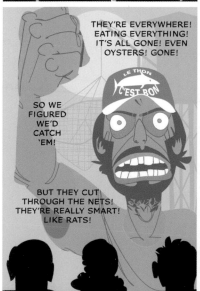

THEY'RE EVERYWHERE! EATING EVERYTHING! IT'S ALL GONE! EVEN OYSTERS! GONE!

SO WE FIGURED WE'D CATCH 'EM!

BUT THEY CUT THROUGH THE NETS! THEY'RE REALLY SMART! LIKE RATS!

LE THON C'EST BON

BUT THE WORST PART IS, THEY'RE EDIBLE!

HEAR THAT, DUMORTIER?

WILL YOU SHUT UP ALREADY?

MAN AND CRUSTACEAN ARE NOW...AT WAR!

NO KIDDING.

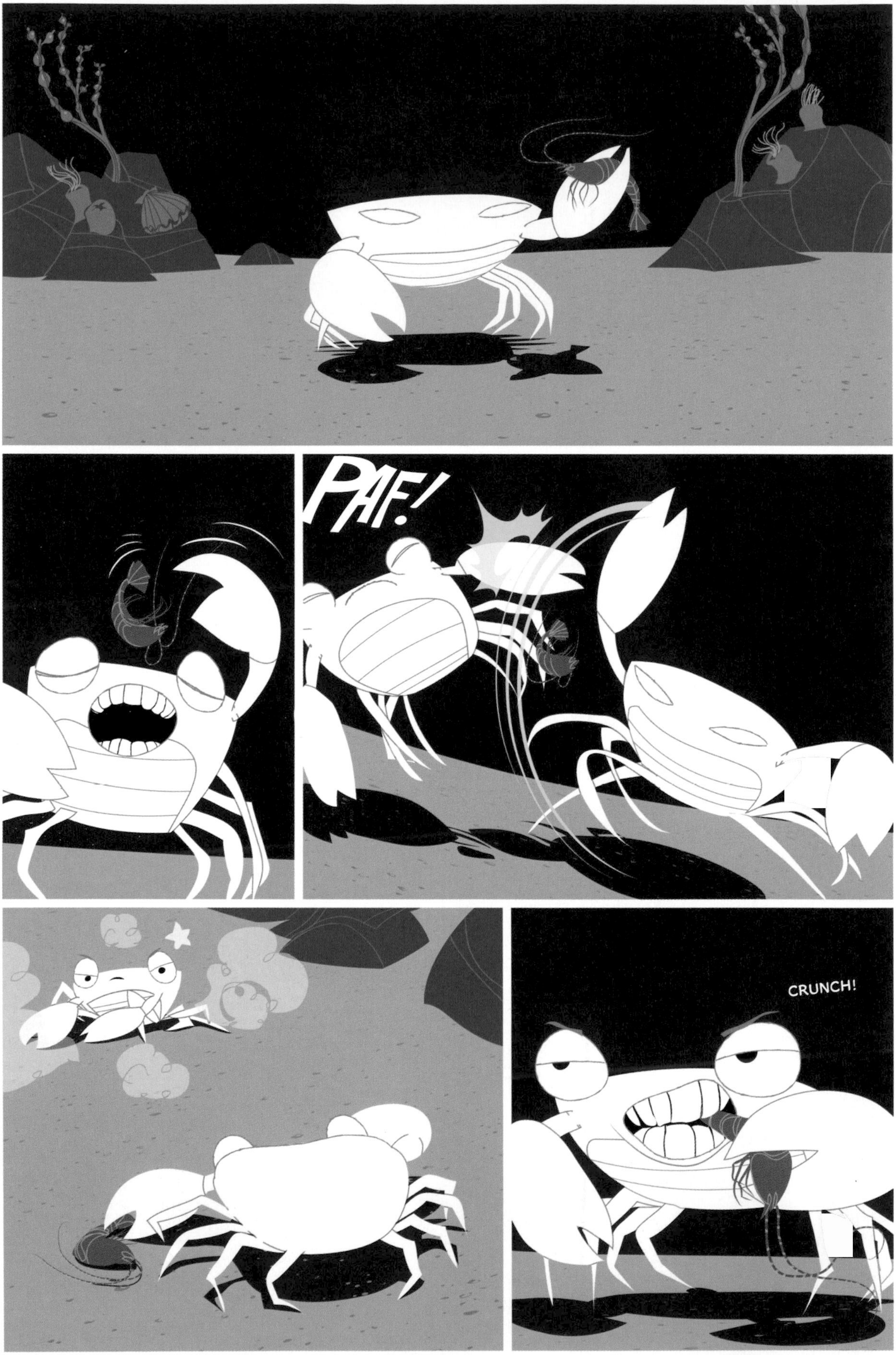
PAF!
CRUNCH!

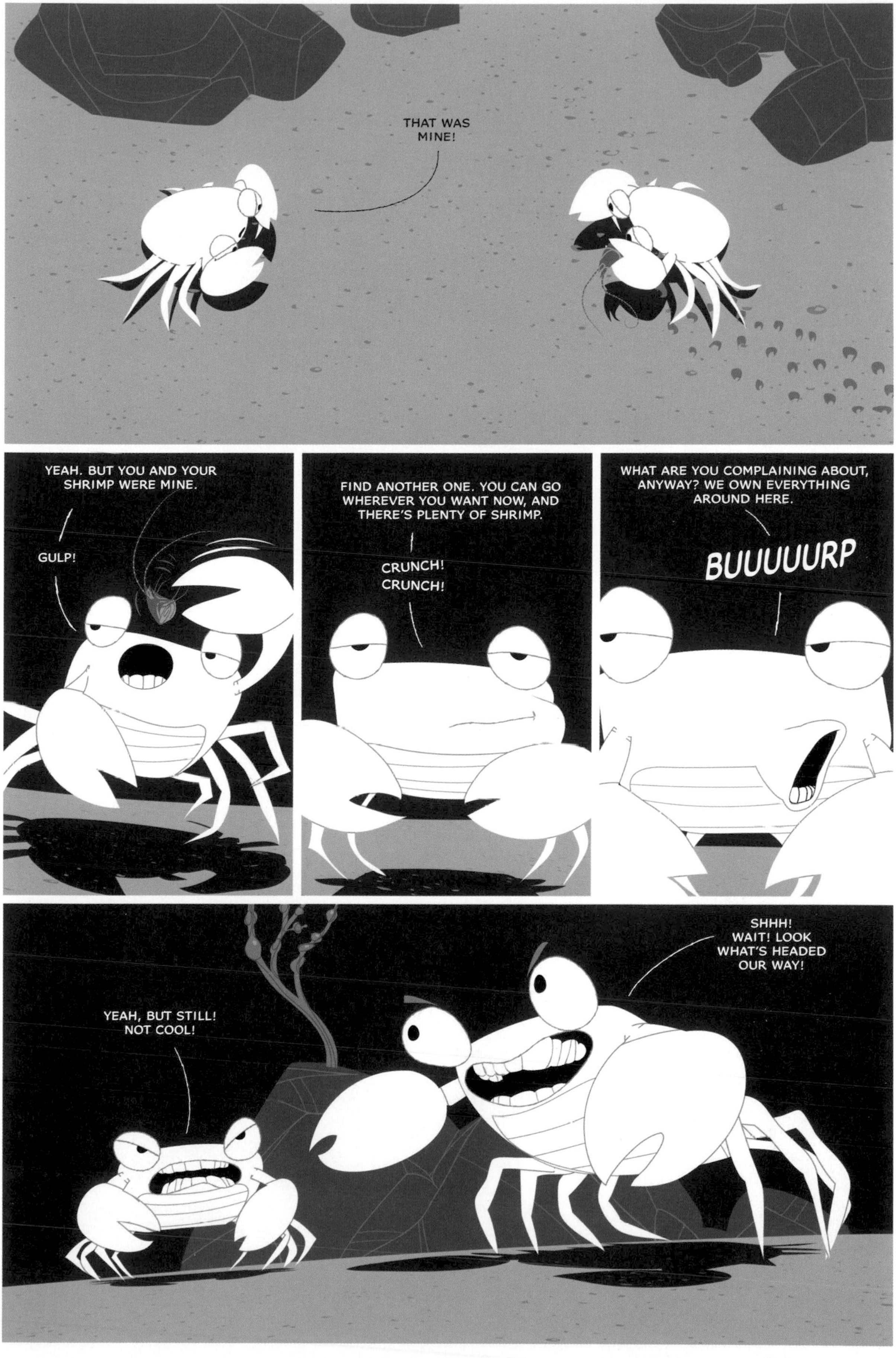
THAT WAS MINE!
YEAH. BUT YOU AND YOUR SHRIMP WERE MINE.
GULP!
FIND ANOTHER ONE. YOU CAN GO WHEREVER YOU WANT NOW, AND THERE'S PLENTY OF SHRIMP.
CRUNCH! CRUNCH!
WHAT ARE YOU COMPLAINING ABOUT, ANYWAY? WE OWN EVERYTHING AROUND HERE.
BUUUUURP
SHHH! WAIT! LOOK WHAT'S HEADED OUR WAY!
YEAH, BUT STILL! NOT COOL!

LET'S HAVE OURSELVES A LITTLE FUN.
WELL, WELL! A RELIC FROM ANOTHER ERA!
HELLO, "BROTHER"! WELL? HOW'D YOU SURVIVE THE OIL SPILL?
AW, C'MON, FELLAS! LEAVE ME ALONE. LET ME CRAWL MY WAY IN PEACE. I'M NOT BOTHERING ANYONE.
NOOOO!
PUT ME DOWN! PLEEEAASE!
YOU GOT IT, PAL!

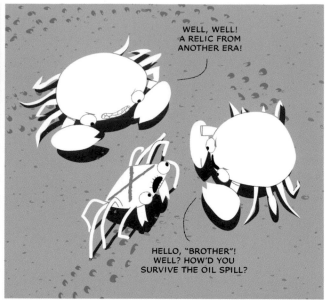

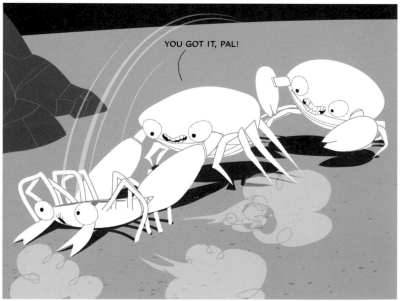

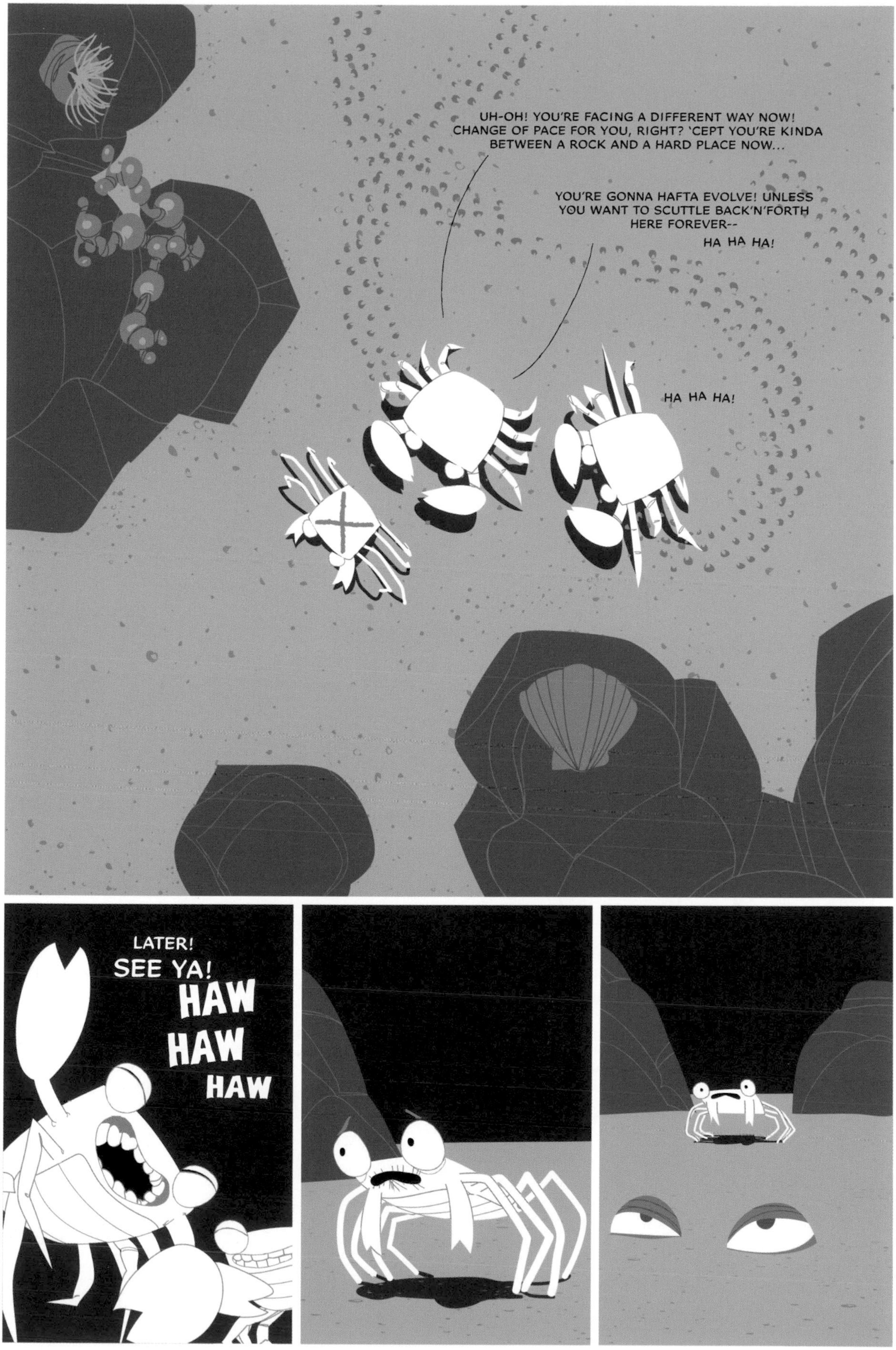
UH-OH! YOU'RE FACING A DIFFERENT WAY NOW! CHANGE OF PACE FOR YOU, RIGHT? 'CEPT YOU'RE KINDA BETWEEN A ROCK AND A HARD PLACE NOW...
YOU'RE GONNA HAFTA EVOLVE! UNLESS YOU WANT TO SCUTTLE BACK'N'FORTH HERE FOREVER--
HA HA HA!
HA HA HA!
LATER!
SEE YA!
HAW
HAW
HAW

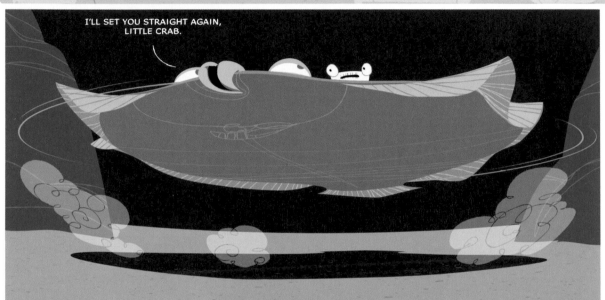

I'LL SET YOU STRAIGHT AGAIN, LITTLE CRAB.

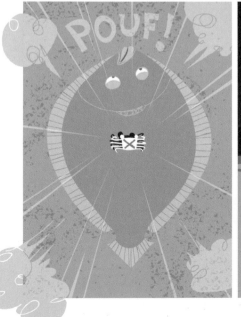

POUF!

THANKS, SOLE!

ANYTIME! I ALREADY MISS THE DAYS WHEN YOUR KIND COULD ONLY MOVE IN A STRAIGHT LINE.

THE MARBLED CRABS HAVE GONE MAD. ALL CREATURES OF THE SEA HAVE GONE MAD.

EVEN SOME SOLES HAVE LET EVOLUTION FEVER OVERTAKE THEM.

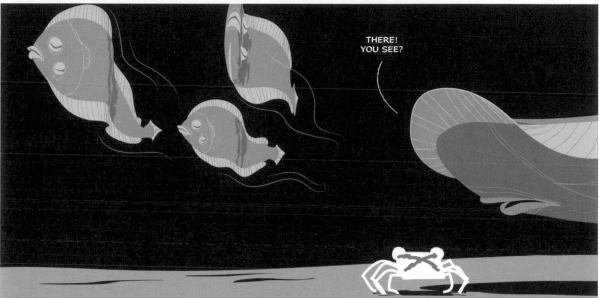

THERE! YOU SEE?

WELL, I KEEP ON WALKING MY LINE! I REMAIN FAITHFUL TO MY VALUES!

THAT IS TO YOUR CREDIT, OLD CRAB.

BUT THIS IS NO OCEAN FOR FOSSILS LIKE US ANYMORE.

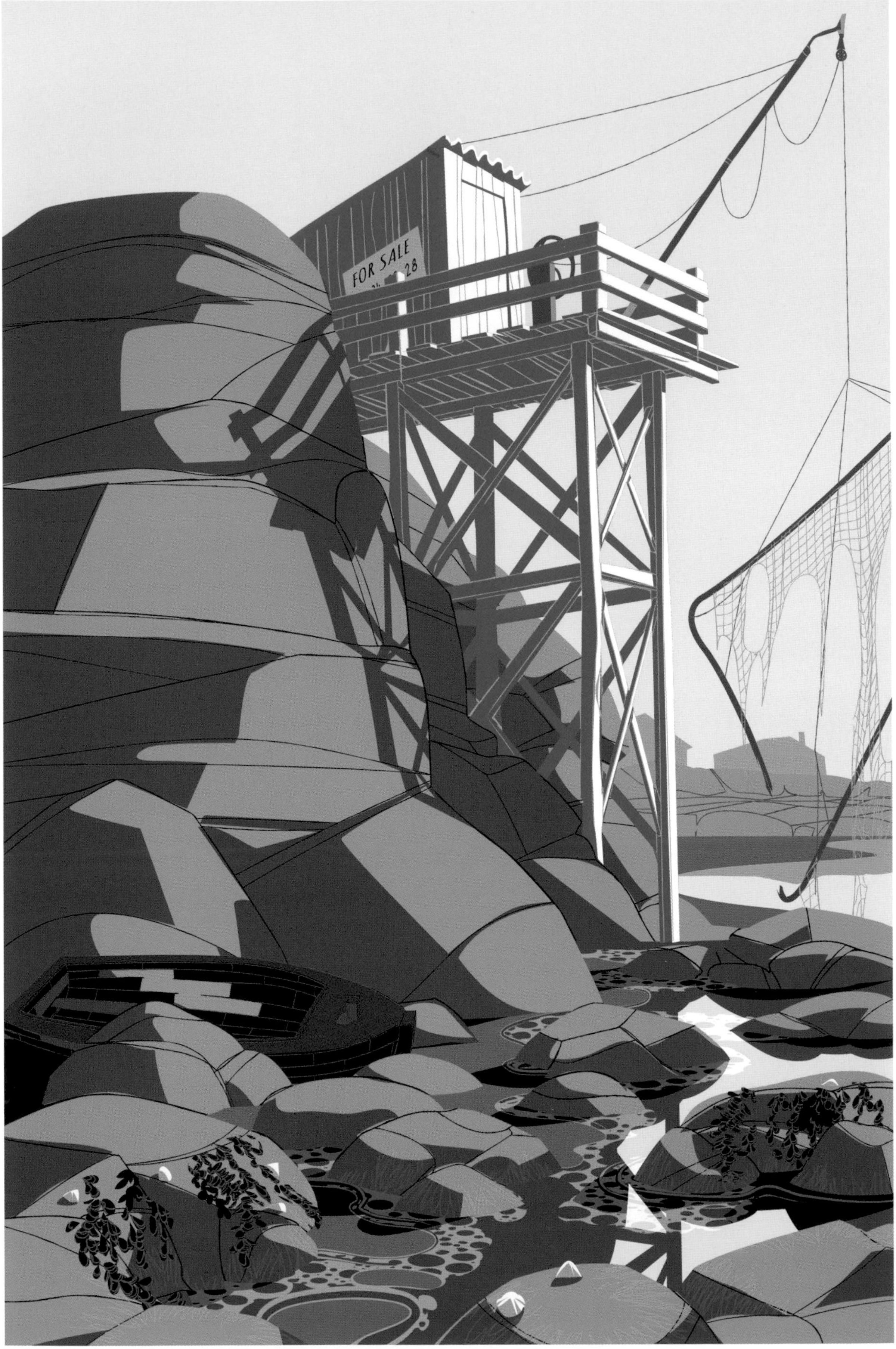
FOR SALE

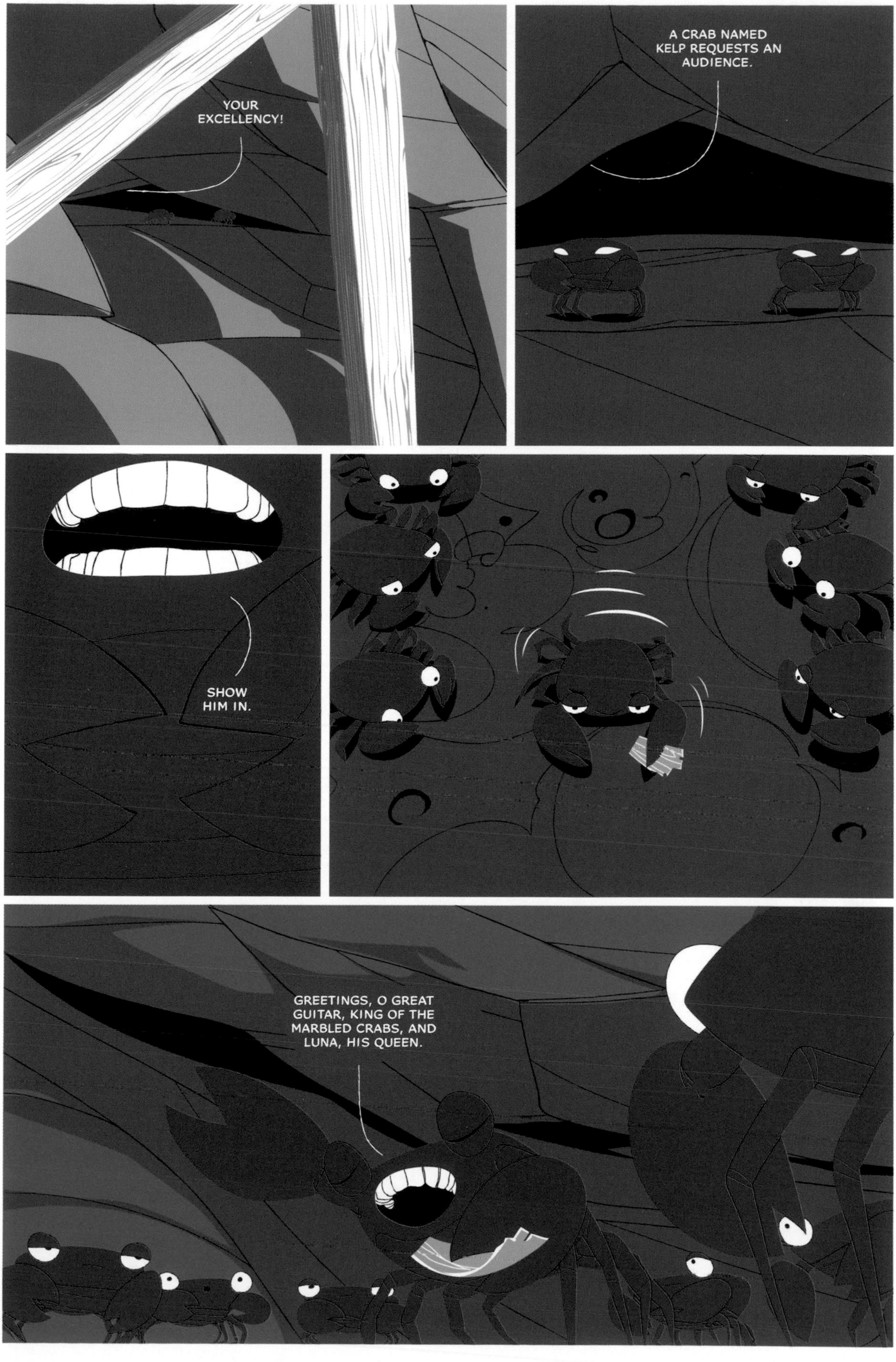
YOUR EXCELLENCY!
A CRAB NAMED KELP REQUESTS AN AUDIENCE.
SHOW HIM IN.
GREETINGS, O GREAT GUITAR, KING OF THE MARBLED CRABS, AND LUNA, HIS QUEEN.

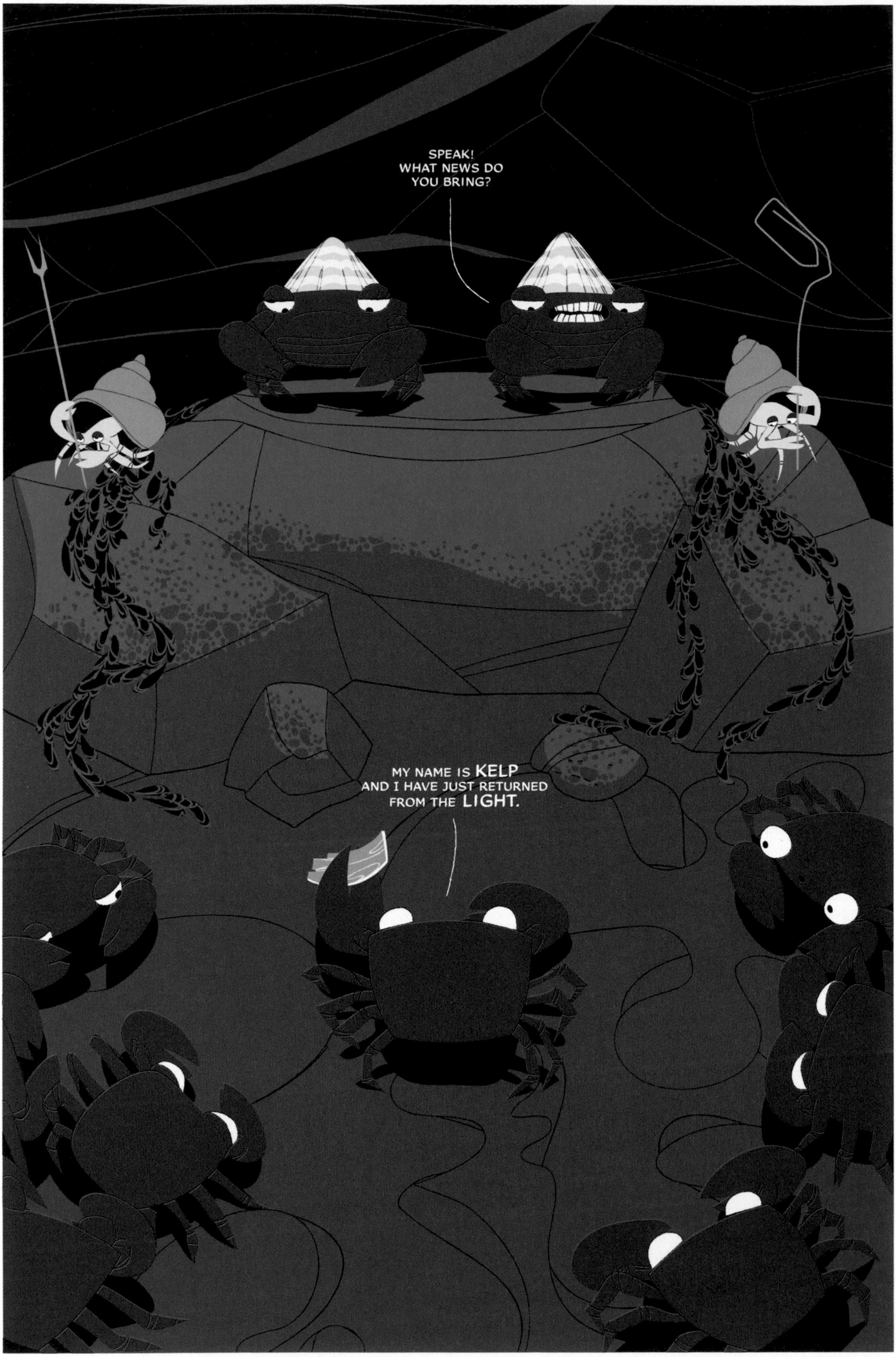
SPEAK!
WHAT NEWS DO
YOU BRING?
MY NAME IS KELP
AND I HAVE JUST RETURNED
FROM THE LIGHT.

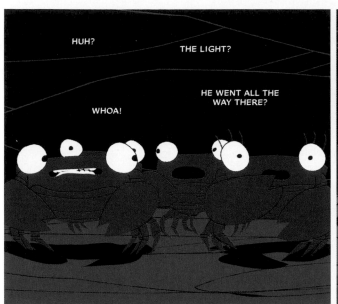

HUH?

THE LIGHT?

WHOA!

HE WENT ALL THE WAY THERE?

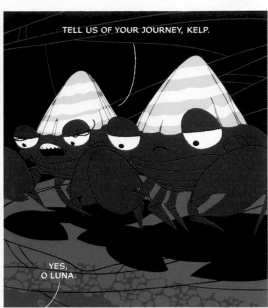

TELL US OF YOUR JOURNEY, KELP.

YES, O LUNA.

A FORTNIGHT AGO, WHEN THE LIGHT FIRST APPEARED IN THE DISTANCE, WHERE THE SEA ENDS...

...OUR BELOVED GUIDE SUNNY, ACCOMPANIED BY TWENTY-TWO OF US, EMBARKED ON A VOYAGE OF EXPLORATION.

ONE WEEK AGO, WHEN NONE OF THEM HAD RETURNED, I RESOLVED TO SET OUT IN TURN.

KELP! DON'T GO!

I'LL BE BACK IN TIME FOR DINNER, SWEETIE!

BEING OF SOUND MIND AND BODY, AND DESIROUS OF A CHALLENGE, I SET OUT FOR ADVENTURE.

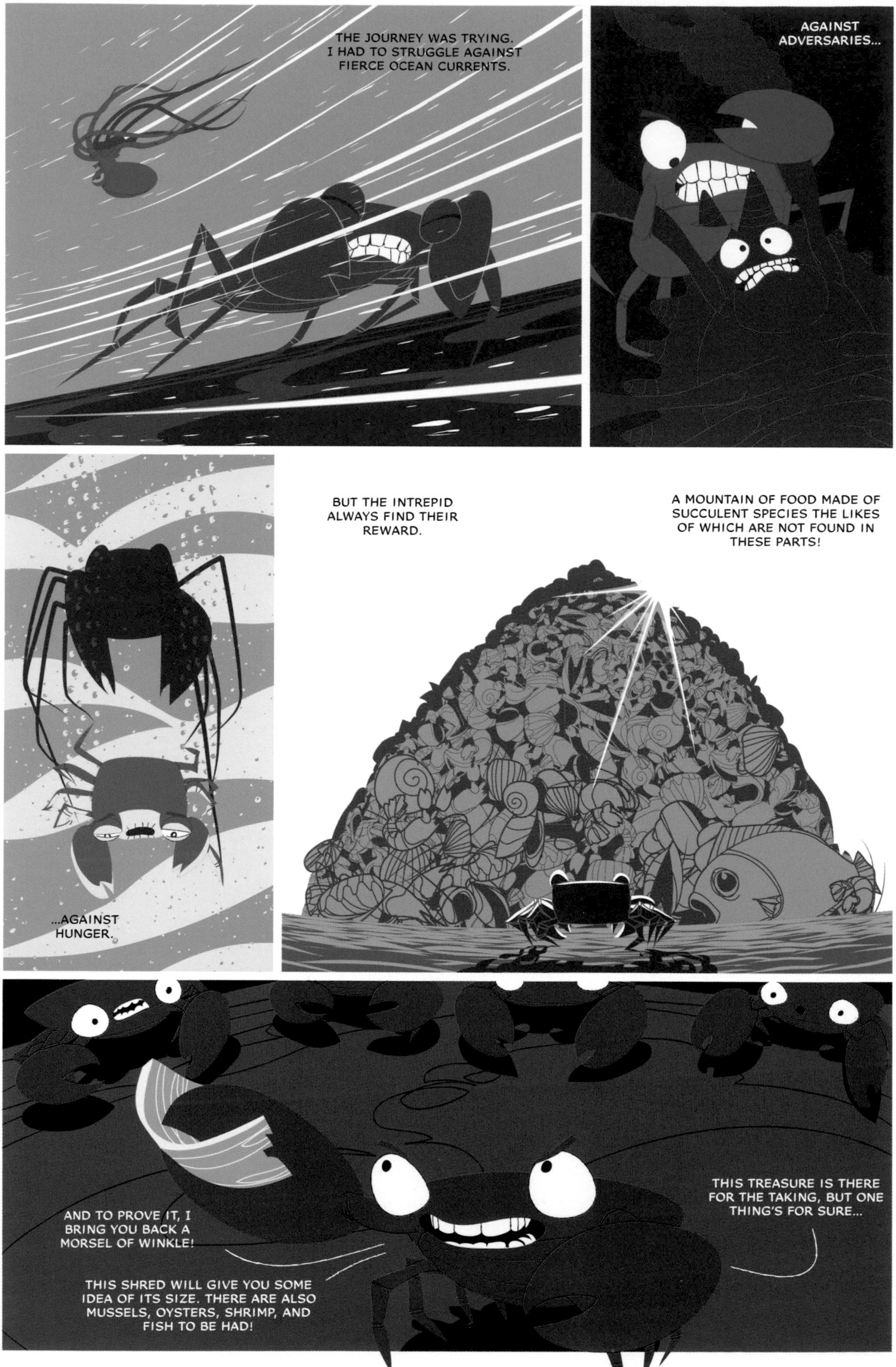
THE JOURNEY WAS TRYING. I HAD TO STRUGGLE AGAINST FIERCE OCEAN CURRENTS.
AGAINST ADVERSARIES...
...AGAINST HUNGER.
BUT THE INTREPID ALWAYS FIND THEIR REWARD.
A MOUNTAIN OF FOOD MADE OF SUCCULENT SPECIES THE LIKES OF WHICH ARE NOT FOUND IN THESE PARTS!
AND TO PROVE IT, I BRING YOU BACK A MORSEL OF WINKLE!
THIS SHRED WILL GIVE YOU SOME IDEA OF ITS SIZE. THERE ARE ALSO MUSSELS, OYSTERS, SHRIMP, AND FISH TO BE HAD!
THIS TREASURE IS THERE FOR THE TAKING, BUT ONE THING'S FOR SURE...

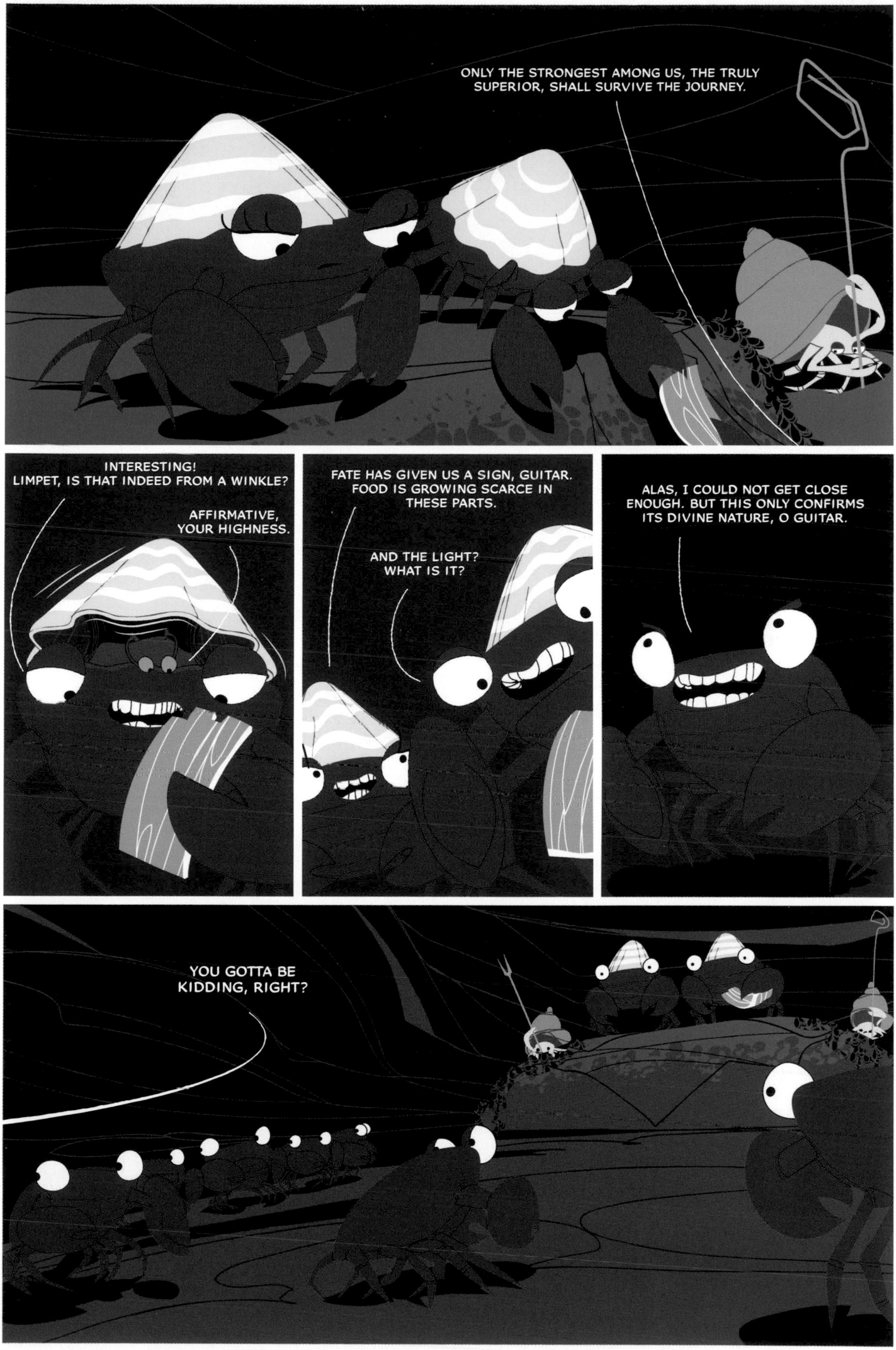
ONLY THE STRONGEST AMONG US, THE TRULY SUPERIOR, SHALL SURVIVE THE JOURNEY.
INTERESTING! LIMPET, IS THAT INDEED FROM A WINKLE?
AFFIRMATIVE, YOUR HIGHNESS.
FATE HAS GIVEN US A SIGN, GUITAR. FOOD IS GROWING SCARCE IN THESE PARTS.
AND THE LIGHT? WHAT IS IT?
ALAS, I COULD NOT GET CLOSE ENOUGH. BUT THIS ONLY CONFIRMS ITS DIVINE NATURE, O GUITAR.
YOU GOTTA BE KIDDING, RIGHT?

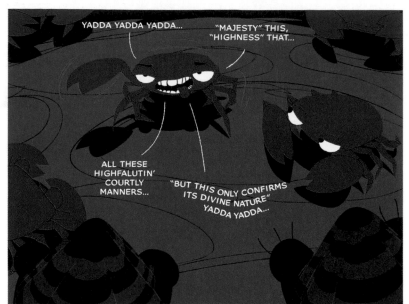

YADDA YADDA YADDA... "MAJESTY" THIS, "HIGHNESS" THAT...

ALL THESE HIGHFALUTIN' COURTLY MANNERS...

"BUT THIS ONLY CONFIRMS ITS DIVINE NATURE" YADDA YADDA...

GUITAR! WHAT IS THIS INSANITY?

WE DON'T EVEN KNOW WHAT THE LIGHT IS!

AND SUNNY STILL HASN'T COME BACK!

TALK ABOUT CHICKEN OF THE SEA!

SUCH DISPLAYS OF FATALISM ARE TYPICAL OF INFERIOR SPECIMENS. THEY KNOW THEY'LL NEVER REACH THE LIGHT.

SAY WHAT?!!

YOU HEARD ME. INFERIOR.

LOOK LEFT. MISSING SOMETHING, AREN'T YOU?

PAF!

LITTLE TURD!

I LOST A CLAW FIGHTING OFF THREE BROWN CRABS SO RUNTLINGS LIKE YOU COULD SCHLEP YOU SHELLS AROUND FREE FEAR!
DON'T YOU COME AT ME TALKING ABOUT "INFERIORITY"!
INFERIOR SHMINFERIOR! GUITAR--
BOATER, YOU'RE BEING VULGAR.
KELP, YOU ARE YOUNG AND HOT-TEMPERED. SEE TO IT THAT YOU DO NOT DISRESPECT A HERO OF THE REVOLUTION.
WRECK!
MUS SEL-BRAIN!
BUT YOUR TALE IS OF GREAT INTEREST TO OUR PEOPLE, AND PERHAPS ONE DAY YOU TOO SHALL BE A GREAT CRAB.
AND ON THAT DAY, YOU MAY INSULT WHOMEVER YOU WISH.
KELP, THANKS TO YOU, A NEW STAGE IN OUR, ER...
EVOLUTION, SIRE.
EVOLUTION IS ABOUT TO BEGIN!
ONLY THE FITTEST CRABS SHALL EARN THE RIGHT TO SURVIVE!

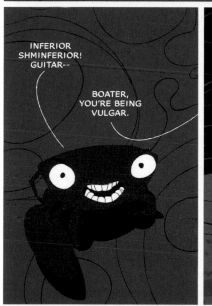

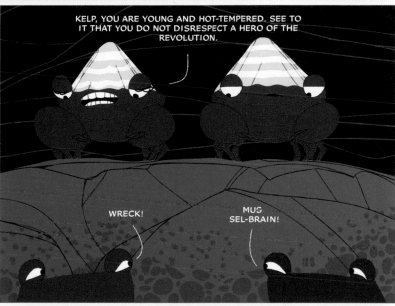

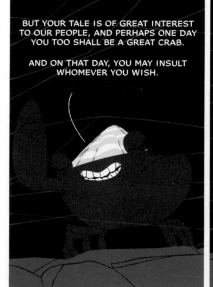

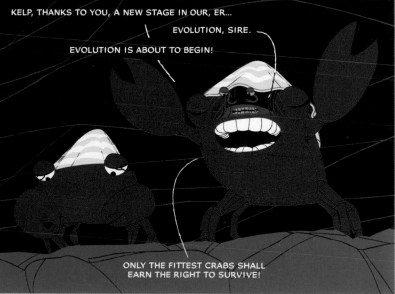

I HAVE DUBBED THIS PHENOMENON "NATURAL SECRETION"--
SELECTION!
GUITAR! WHY, YOU--
YOU'VE LOST YOUR MIND!
I'VE HAD IT WITH YOU "SUPERIOR" TYPES! GOOD RIDDANCE!
POOR BOATER! WHO KNOWS? PERHAPS ONE DAY HE TOO SHALL ESTABLISH A NEW SPECIES.
A SPECIES WITH BUT ONE GIANT CLAW, LIKE THE FIDDLER CRAB.
TOO BAD HIS CLAW DIDN'T GROW BACK.
HE COULD'VE BEEN ONE OF US.

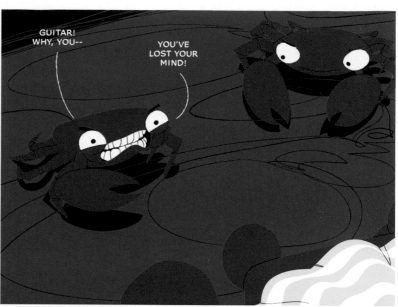

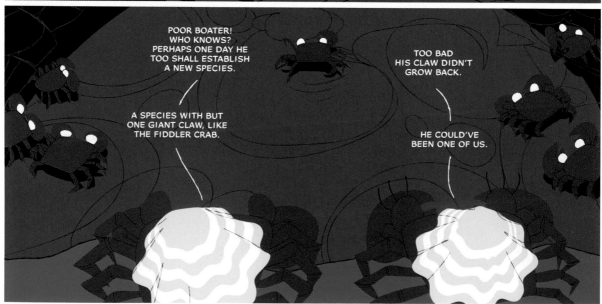

BUNCH OF MORONS!
BUNCH OF MORONS!
BUNCH OF MORONS!
BUNCH OF MORONS!
O, LIGHT!
YOU ARE OUR GUIDE. WE ENTRUST OUR FATE TO YOU.
BROTHERS AND SISTERS...
LET US KNEEL!

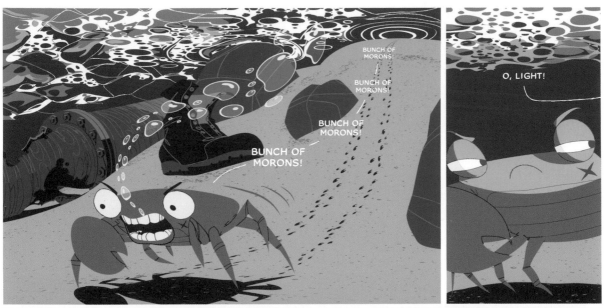

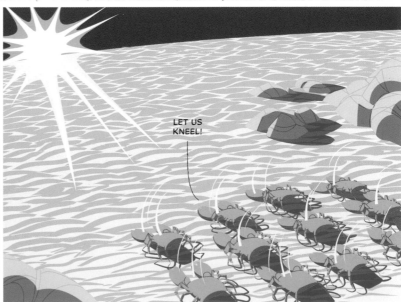

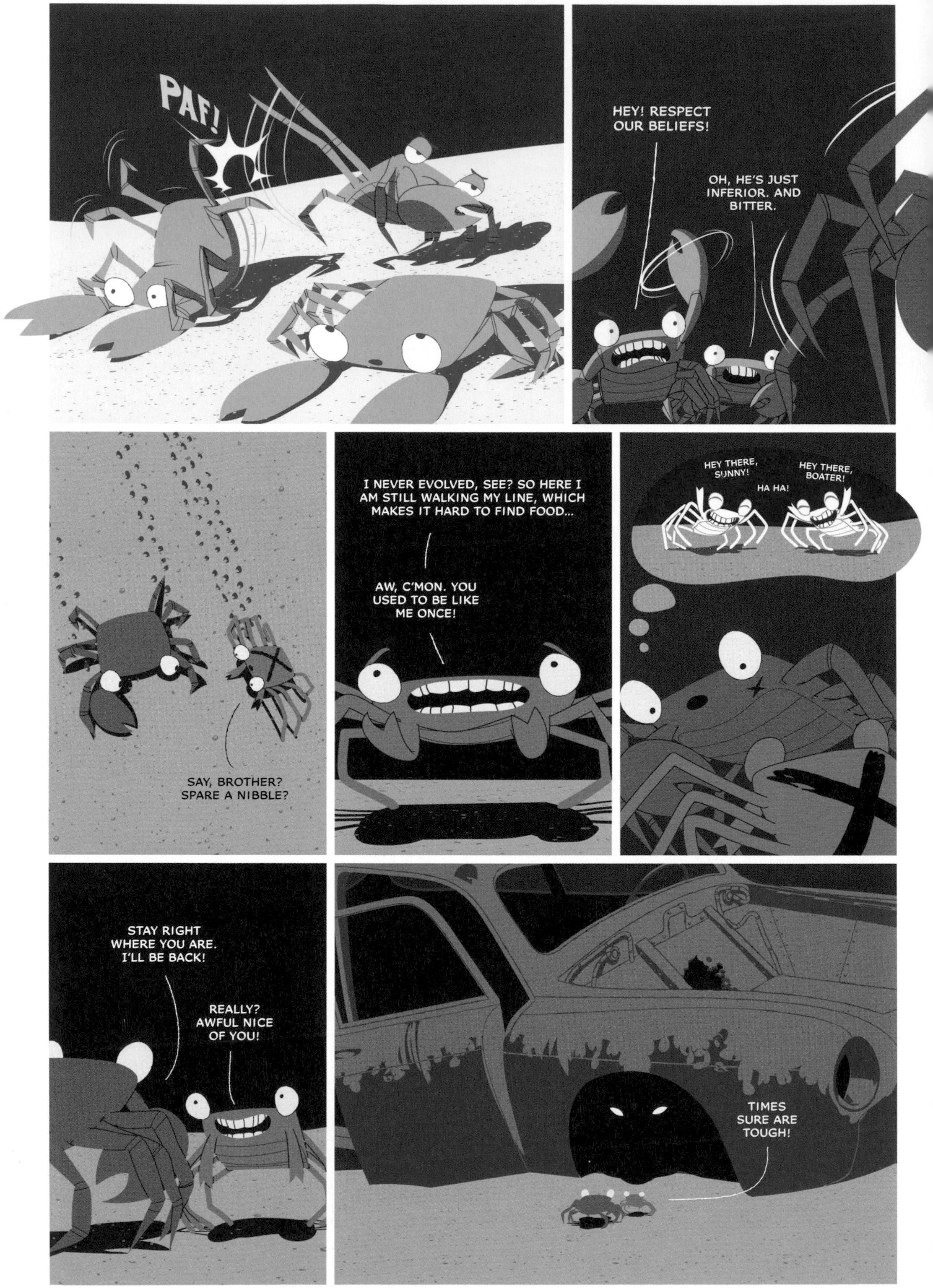
PAF!
HEY! RESPECT OUR BELIEFS!
OH, HE'S JUST INFERIOR. AND BITTER.
SAY, BROTHER? SPARE A NIBBLE?
I NEVER EVOLVED, SEE? SO HERE I AM STILL WALKING MY LINE, WHICH MAKES IT HARD TO FIND FOOD...
AW, C'MON. YOU USED TO BE LIKE ME ONCE!
HEY THERE, SUNNY!
HA HA!
HEY THERE, BOATER!
STAY RIGHT WHERE YOU ARE. I'LL BE BACK!
REALLY? AWFUL NICE OF YOU!
TIMES SURE ARE TOUGH!

CLAP!

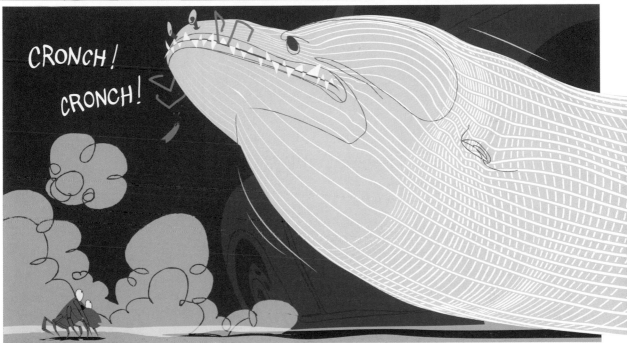

CRONCH!

CRONCH!

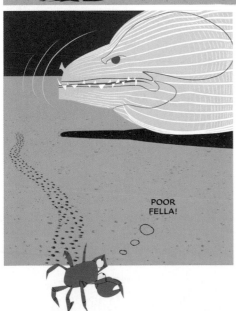

POOR
FELLA!

I DON'T KNOW WHERE
CRAB SOULS GO, BUT I
HOPE HE DOESN'T HAVE TO
WALK THE LINE FOR ALL
ETERNITY!

TIMES
SURE ARE
TOUGH...

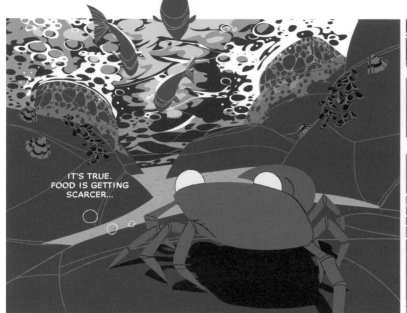

IT'S TRUE. FOOD IS GETTING SCARCER...

NO MORE OYSTERS...

SHRIMP'RE ALMOST GONE...

BASTARD! TAKE THAT!

THIEF!

I HEAR SOME CRABS'RE EVEN EATING EACH OTHER!

AAAARGH!

ALL OUR STRUGGLES... AND FOR WHAT?

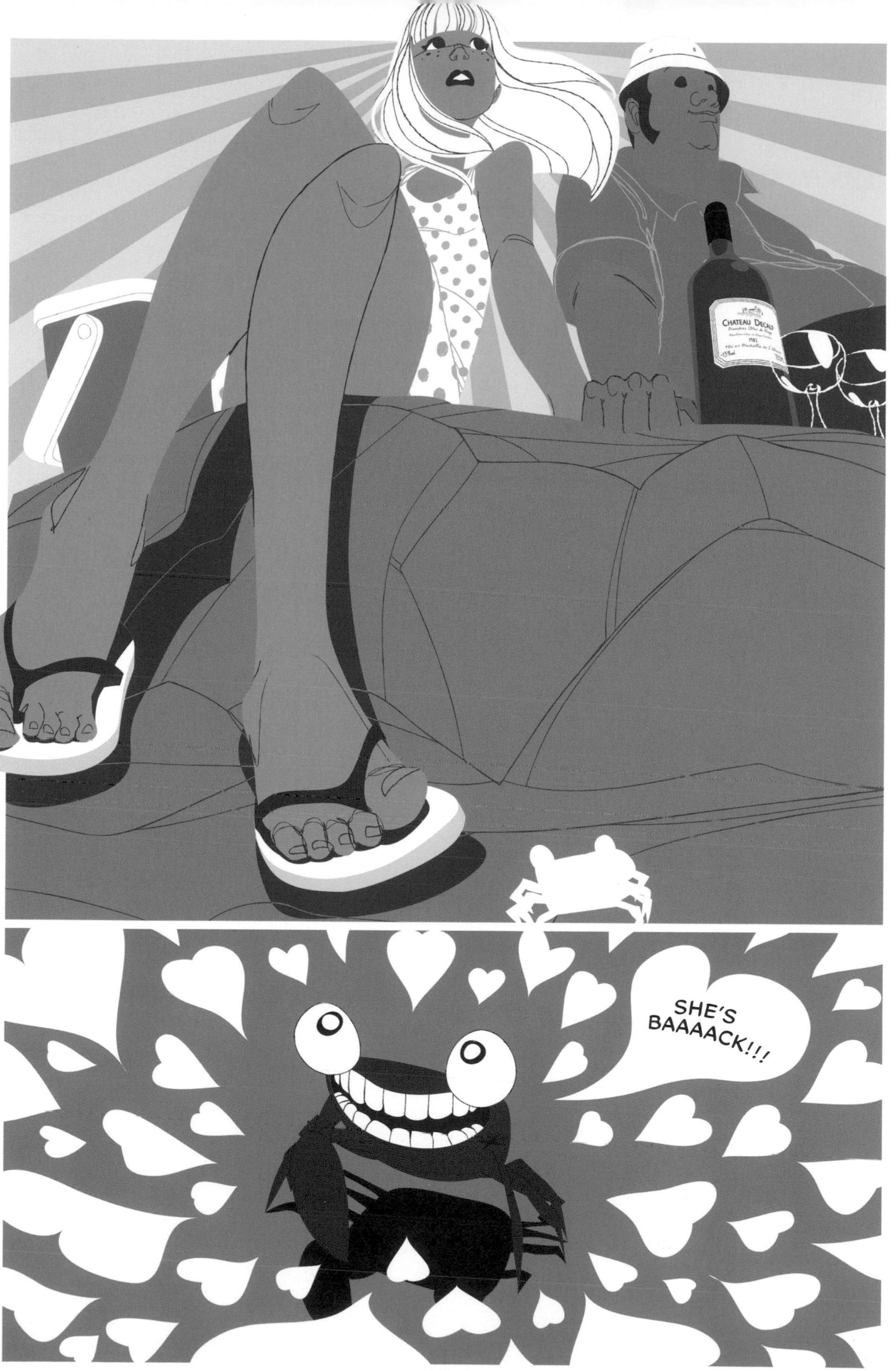
SHE'S BAAAACK!!!

WHY'D YOU MAKE US COME BACK HERE? IT'S FULL OF CRABS AND SMELLS.

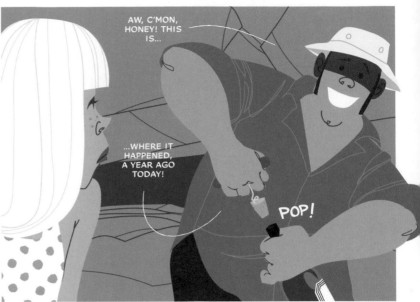

AW, C'MON, HONEY! THIS IS...

...WHERE IT HAPPENED, A YEAR AGO TODAY!

POP!

OH, SILLY ME! THIS IS WHERE WE FIRST MET!

THAT'S RIGHT! I WAS SHOOTING A MOVIE, AND YOU WERE RESCUING A LI'L CRAB...

HMPH! THAT FAT MAN AGAIN!

TO YEAR ONE! TO YEAR ONE!

TING!

UH... SOLANGE?

ACTUALLY, I BROUGHT YOU BACK HERE FOR A SPECIAL REASON...

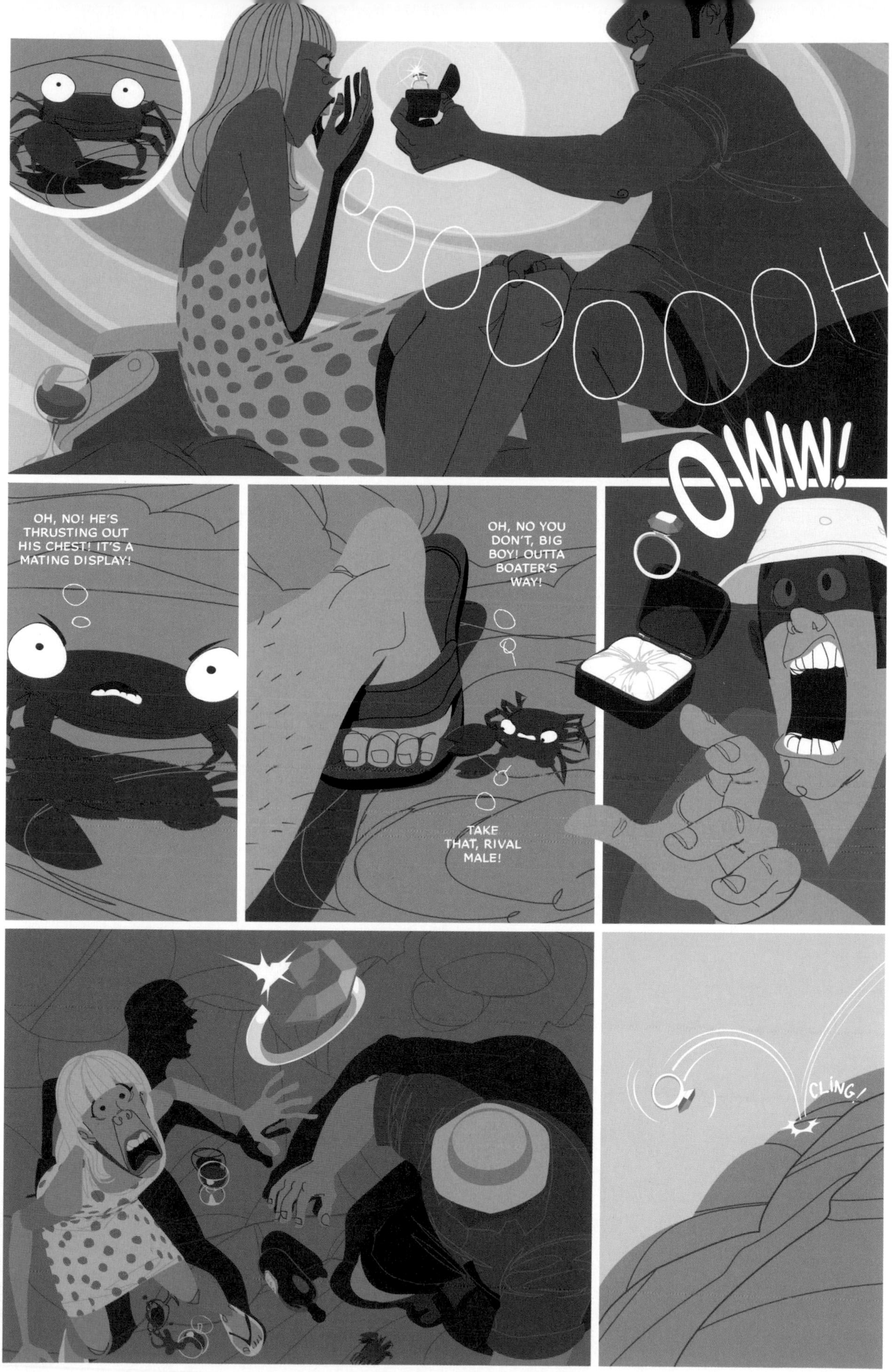
OOOOOOOOOH
OWW!
OH, NO! HE'S THRUSTING OUT HIS CHEST! IT'S A MATING DISPLAY!
OH, NO YOU DON'T, BIG BOY! OUTTA BOATER'S WAY!
TAKE THAT, RIVAL MALE!
CLING!

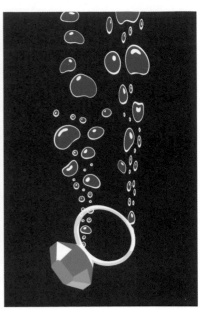

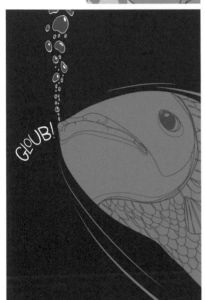

GLOUB!

NOOOOOO !!!

STUPID CRAB!

THAT RING COST TWENTY GRAND!!

HONEY--

STOMP!

STOMP!

MAYBE IT'S A SIGN FROM ABOVE. OUR LOVE WILL LAST FOREVER, JUST AS THAT RING WILL LIE AT THE BOTTOM OF THE SEA FOREVERMORE.

DARLING! THAT'S SO BEAUTIFUL!

CAUTION!

BY ORDER OF THE PREFECTURE, IT IS STRICTLY FORBIDDEN TO:

• FEED CRABS
• CATCH CRABS
• WALK BAREFOOT

MINORS MUST BE ACCOMPANIED BY AN ADULT.

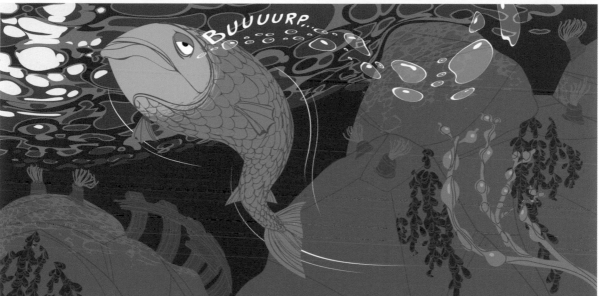

BUUUURP...

I, ROCKY III, SHALL REACH THE LIGHT!

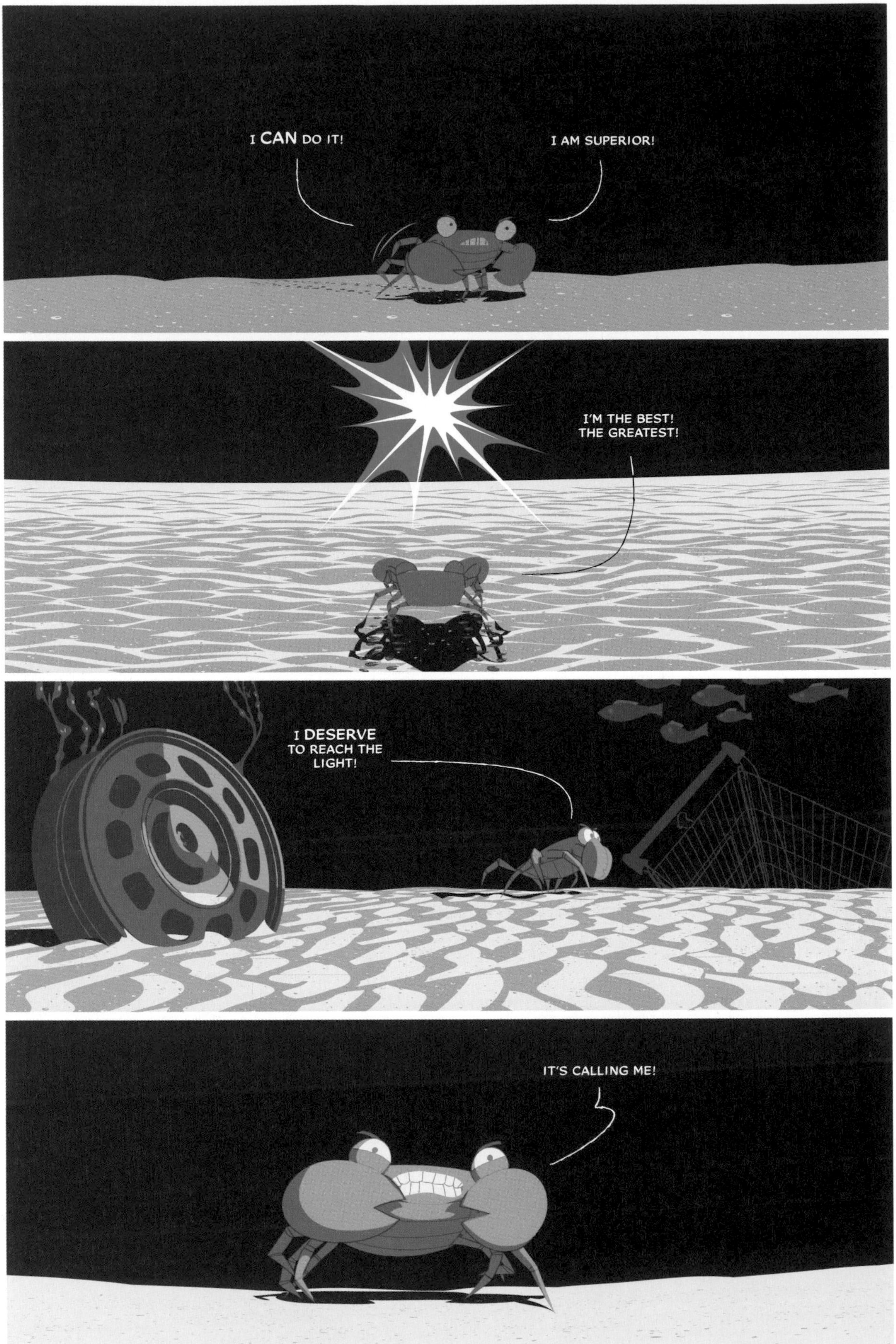
I CAN DO IT!
I AM SUPERIOR!
I'M THE BEST! THE GREATEST!
I DESERVE TO REACH THE LIGHT!
IT'S CALLING ME!

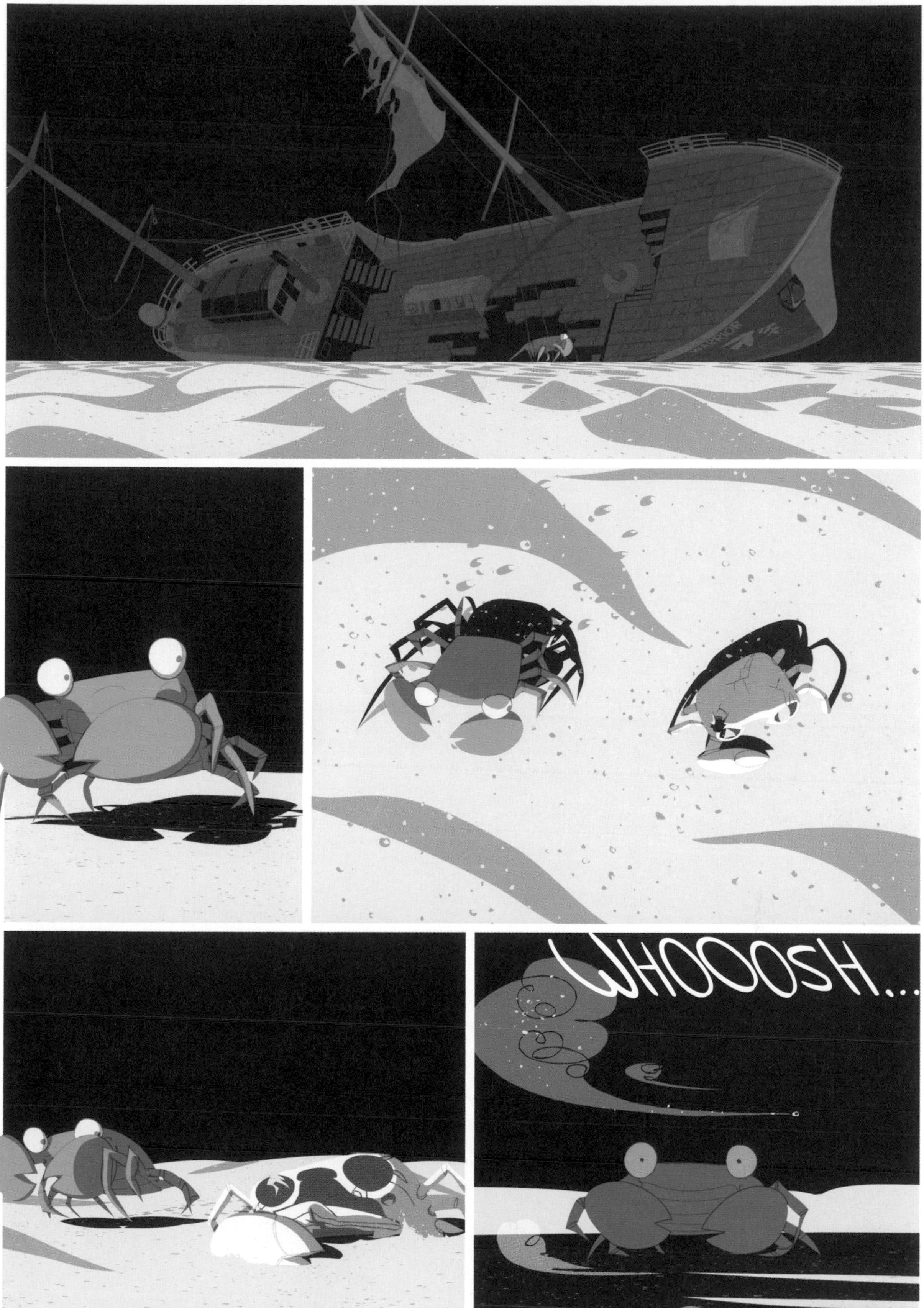
WHOOOSH...

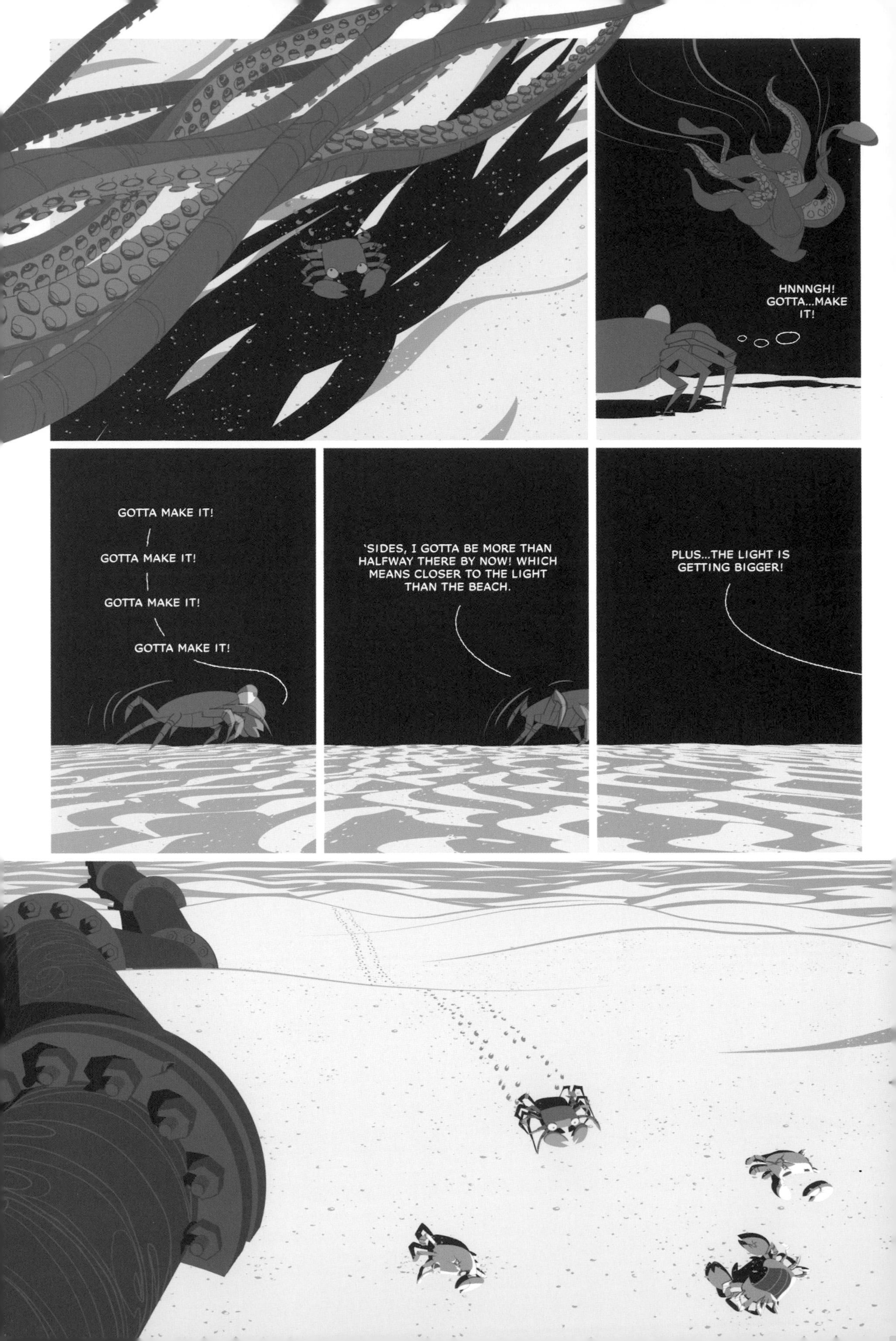
HNNNGH! GOTTA...MAKE IT!
GOTTA MAKE IT!
GOTTA MAKE IT!
GOTTA MAKE IT!
GOTTA MAKE IT!
'SIDES, I GOTTA BE MORE THAN HALFWAY THERE BY NOW! WHICH MEANS CLOSER TO THE LIGHT THAN THE BEACH.
PLUS...THE LIGHT IS GETTING BIGGER!

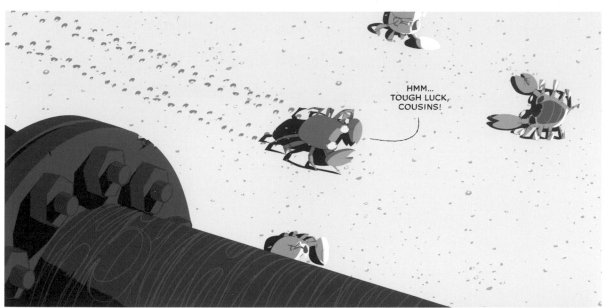

HMM... TOUGH LUCK, COUSINS!

URGH! IT'S GETTING... HARDER...TO BREATH!

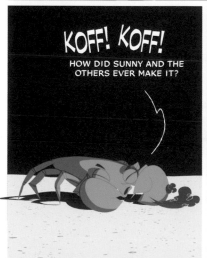

KOFF! KOFF!

HOW DID SUNNY AND THE OTHERS EVER MAKE IT?

HUH?!

OH, NO!

NOT THIS STICKY STUFF AGAIN!

NOOOOO!!!

IT'S JUST NOT FAIR! THE LIGHT...WAS CALLING TO ME!

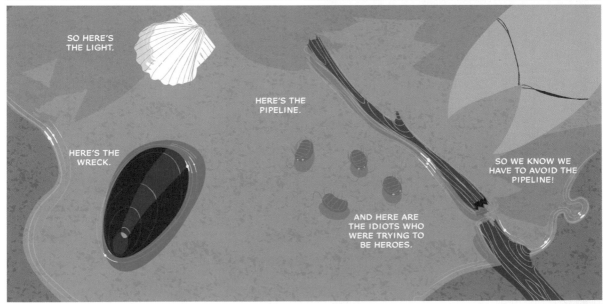

SO HERE'S THE LIGHT.

HERE'S THE PIPELINE.

HERE'S THE WRECK.

AND HERE ARE THE IDIOTS WHO WERE TRYING TO BE HEROES.

SO WE KNOW WE HAVE TO AVOID THE PIPELINE!

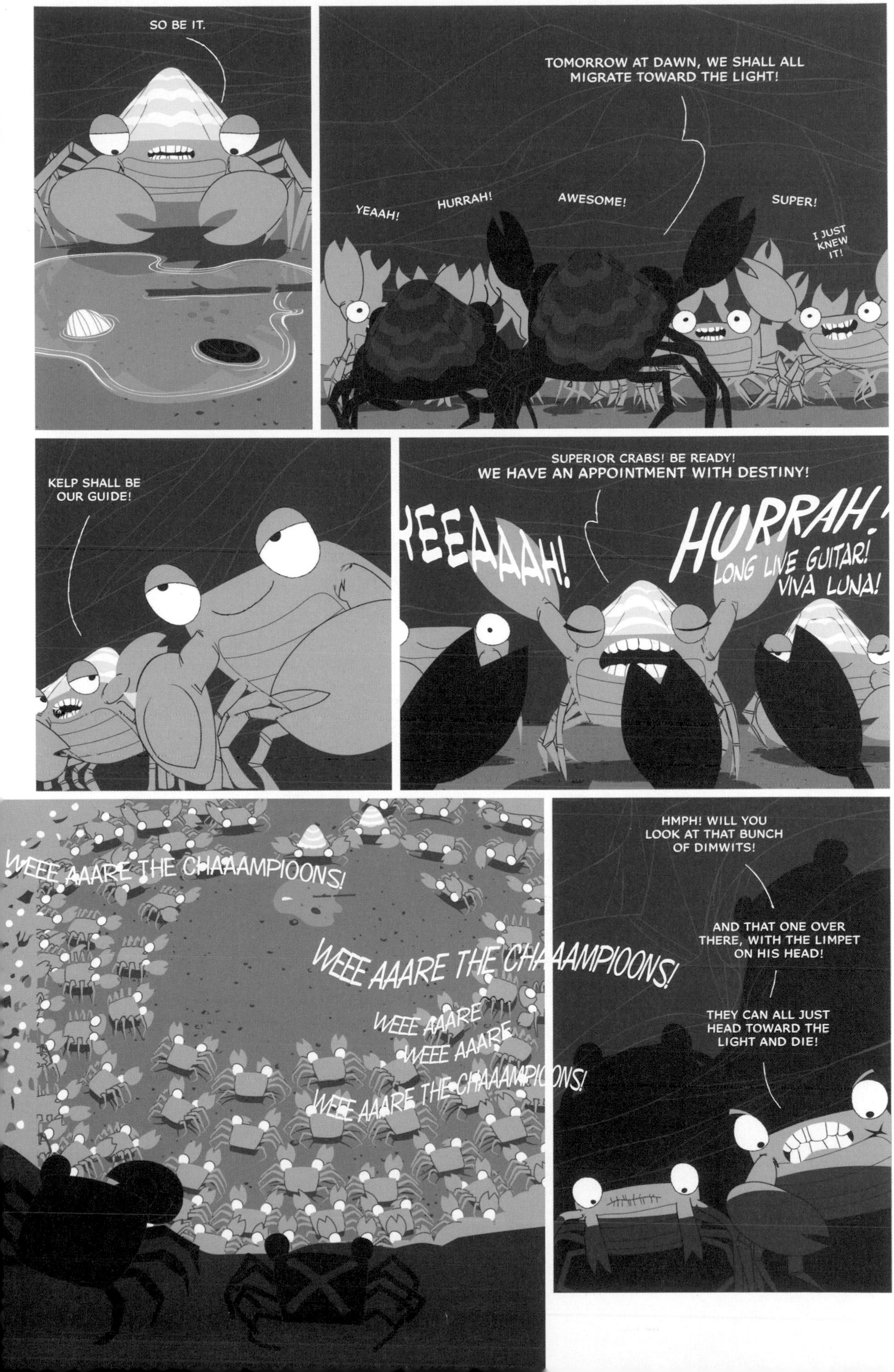
SO BE IT.
TOMORROW AT DAWN, WE SHALL ALL MIGRATE TOWARD THE LIGHT!
YEAAH!
HURRAH!
AWESOME!
SUPER!
I JUST KNEW IT!
KELP SHALL BE OUR GUIDE!
SUPERIOR CRABS! BE READY!
WE HAVE AN APPOINTMENT WITH DESTINY!
YEEAAAH!
HURRAH!
LONG LIVE GUITAR!
VIVA LUNA!
WEEE AAARE THE CHAAAMPIOONS!
WEEE AAARE THE CHAAAMPIOONS!
WEEE AAARE
WEEE AAARE
WEEE AAARE THE CHAAAMPIOONS!
HMPH! WILL YOU LOOK AT THAT BUNCH OF DIMWITS!
AND THAT ONE OVER THERE, WITH THE LIMPET ON HIS HEAD!
THEY CAN ALL JUST HEAD TOWARD THE LIGHT AND DIE!

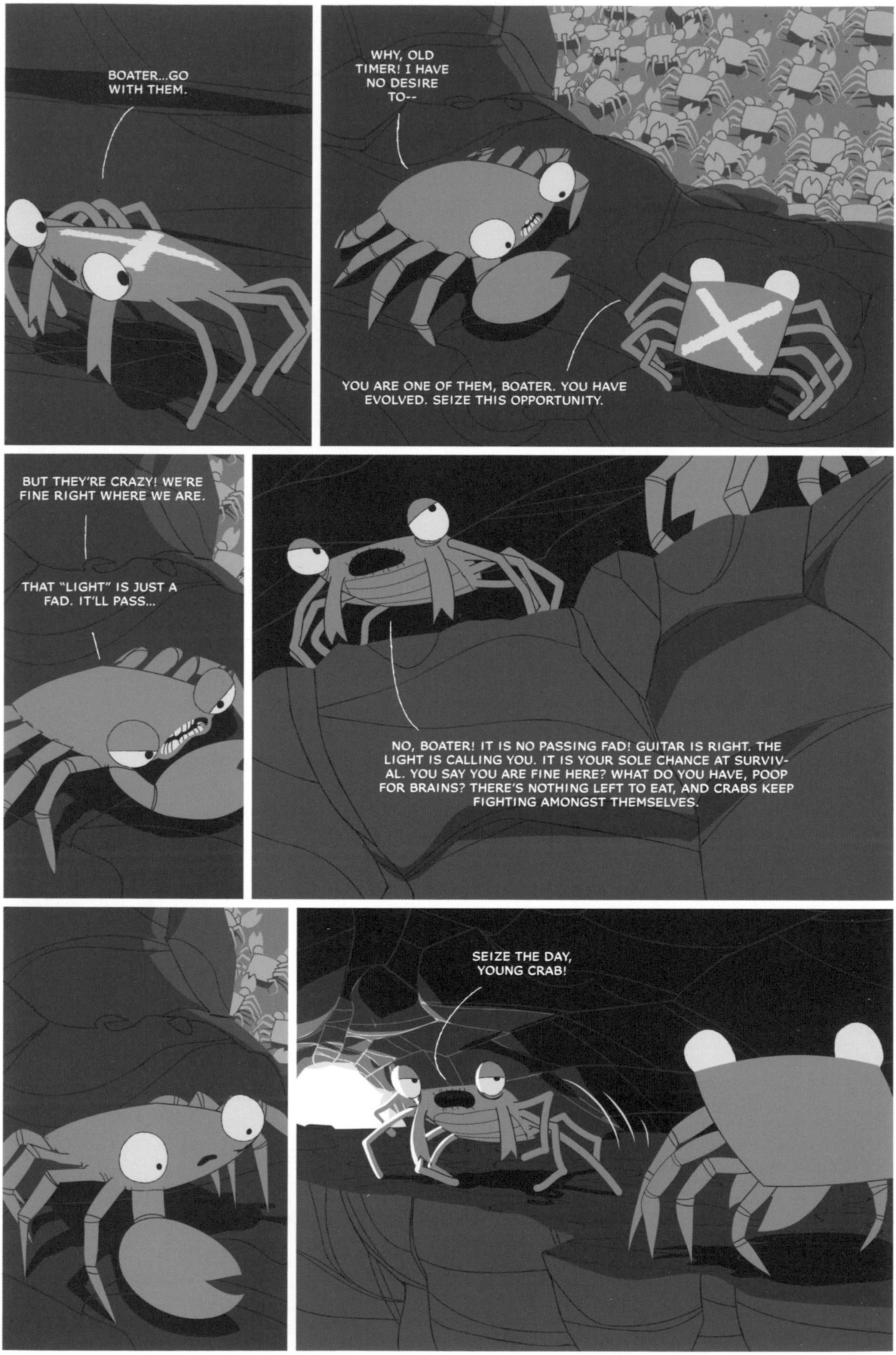
BOATER...GO WITH THEM.
WHY, OLD TIMER! I HAVE NO DESIRE TO--
YOU ARE ONE OF THEM, BOATER. YOU HAVE EVOLVED. SEIZE THIS OPPORTUNITY.
BUT THEY'RE CRAZY! WE'RE FINE RIGHT WHERE WE ARE.
THAT "LIGHT" IS JUST A FAD. IT'LL PASS...
NO, BOATER! IT IS NO PASSING FAD! GUITAR IS RIGHT. THE LIGHT IS CALLING YOU. IT IS YOUR SOLE CHANCE AT SURVIV- AL. YOU SAY YOU ARE FINE HERE? WHAT DO YOU HAVE, POOP FOR BRAINS? THERE'S NOTHING LEFT TO EAT, AND CRABS KEEP FIGHTING AMONGST THEMSELVES.
SEIZE THE DAY, YOUNG CRAB!

YOU'RE RIGHT, OLD TIMER.
I'LL GO WITH THEM.
THINK I CONVINCED HIM.
PERFECT!
ONCE ALL THOSE DIRTY TURNERS ARE GONE, WE'LL RE-POPULATE THIS BEACH!
WE'LL MAKE EVERYTHING RIGHT AGAIN!

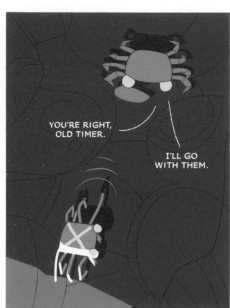

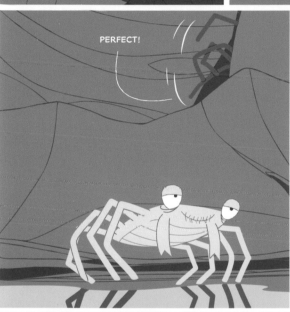

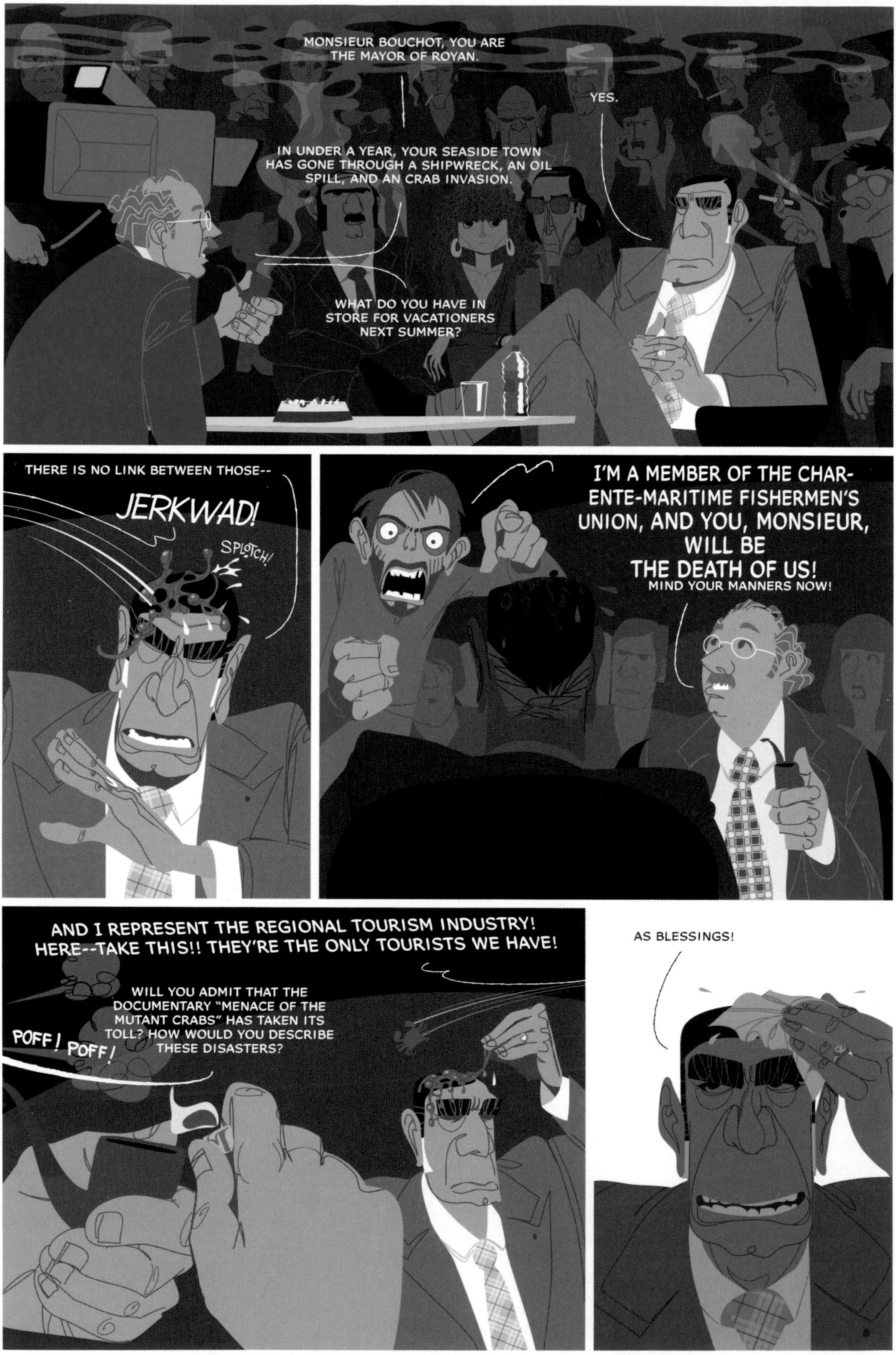
MONSIEUR BOUCHOT, YOU ARE THE MAYOR OF ROYAN.
YES.
IN UNDER A YEAR, YOUR SEASIDE TOWN HAS GONE THROUGH A SHIPWRECK, AN OIL SPILL, AND AN CRAB INVASION.
WHAT DO YOU HAVE IN STORE FOR VACATIONERS NEXT SUMMER?
THERE IS NO LINK BETWEEN THOSE--
JERKWAD!
SPLOTCH!
I'M A MEMBER OF THE CHARENTE-MARITIME FISHERMEN'S UNION, AND YOU, MONSIEUR, WILL BE THE DEATH OF US!
MIND YOUR MANNERS NOW!
AND I REPRESENT THE REGIONAL TOURISM INDUSTRY! HERE--TAKE THIS!! THEY'RE THE ONLY TOURISTS WE HAVE!
WILL YOU ADMIT THAT THE DOCUMENTARY "MENACE OF THE MUTANT CRABS" HAS TAKEN ITS TOLL? HOW WOULD YOU DESCRIBE THESE DISASTERS?
POFF! POFF!
AS BLESSINGS!

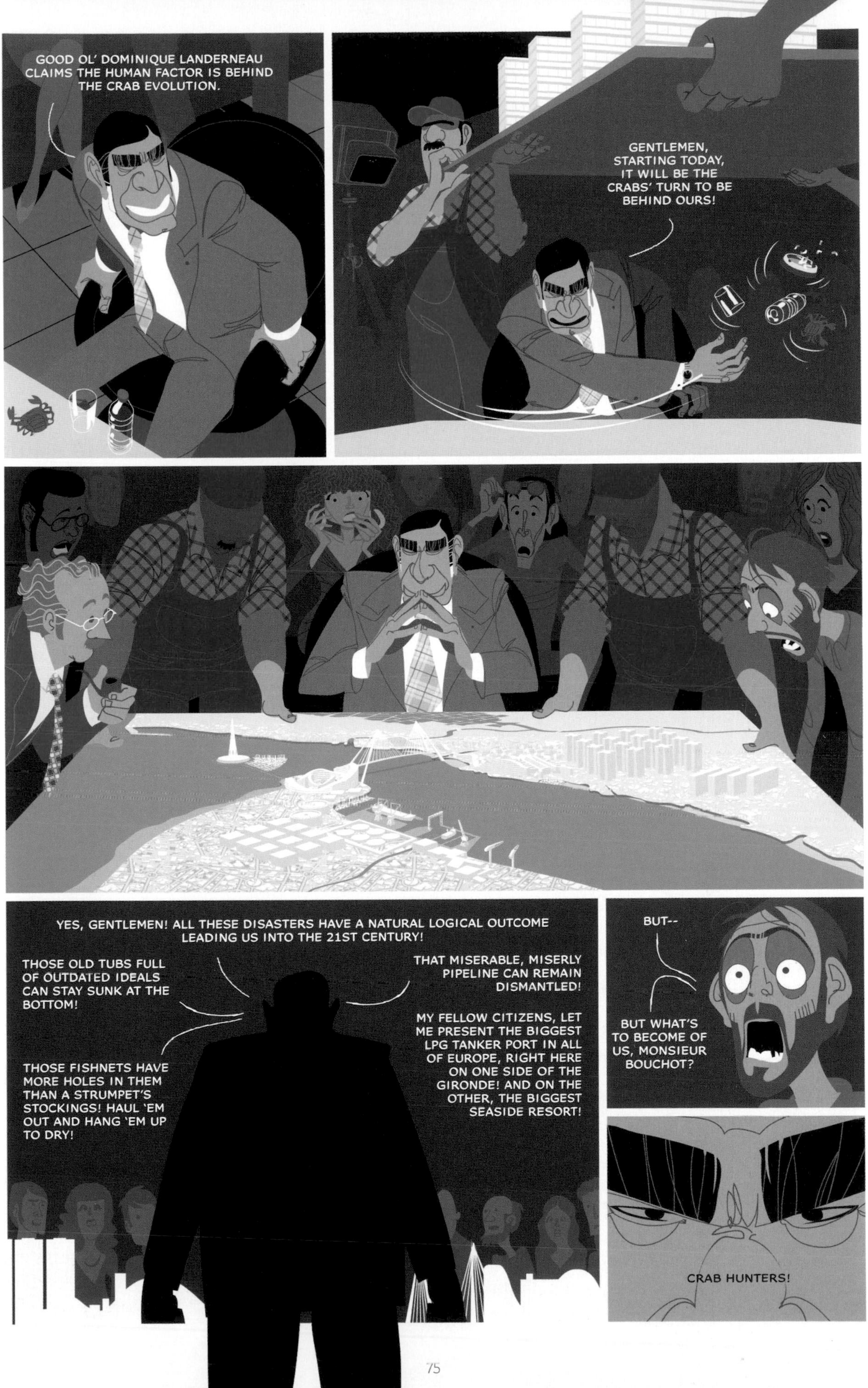
GOOD OL' DOMINIQUE LANDERNEAU CLAIMS THE HUMAN FACTOR IS BEHIND THE CRAB EVOLUTION.
GENTLEMEN, STARTING TODAY, IT WILL BE THE CRABS' TURN TO BE BEHIND OURS!
YES, GENTLEMEN! ALL THESE DISASTERS HAVE A NATURAL LOGICAL OUTCOME LEADING US INTO THE 21ST CENTURY!
THOSE OLD TUBS FULL OF OUTDATED IDEALS CAN STAY SUNK AT THE BOTTOM!
THOSE FISHNETS HAVE MORE HOLES IN THEM THAN A STRUMPET'S STOCKINGS! HAUL 'EM OUT AND HANG 'EM UP TO DRY!
THAT MISERABLE, MISERLY PIPELINE CAN REMAIN DISMANTLED!
MY FELLOW CITIZENS, LET ME PRESENT THE BIGGEST LPG TANKER PORT IN ALL OF EUROPE, RIGHT HERE ON ONE SIDE OF THE GIRONDE! AND ON THE OTHER, THE BIGGEST SEASIDE RESORT!
BUT--
BUT WHAT'S TO BECOME OF US, MONSIEUR BOUCHOT?
CRAB HUNTERS!

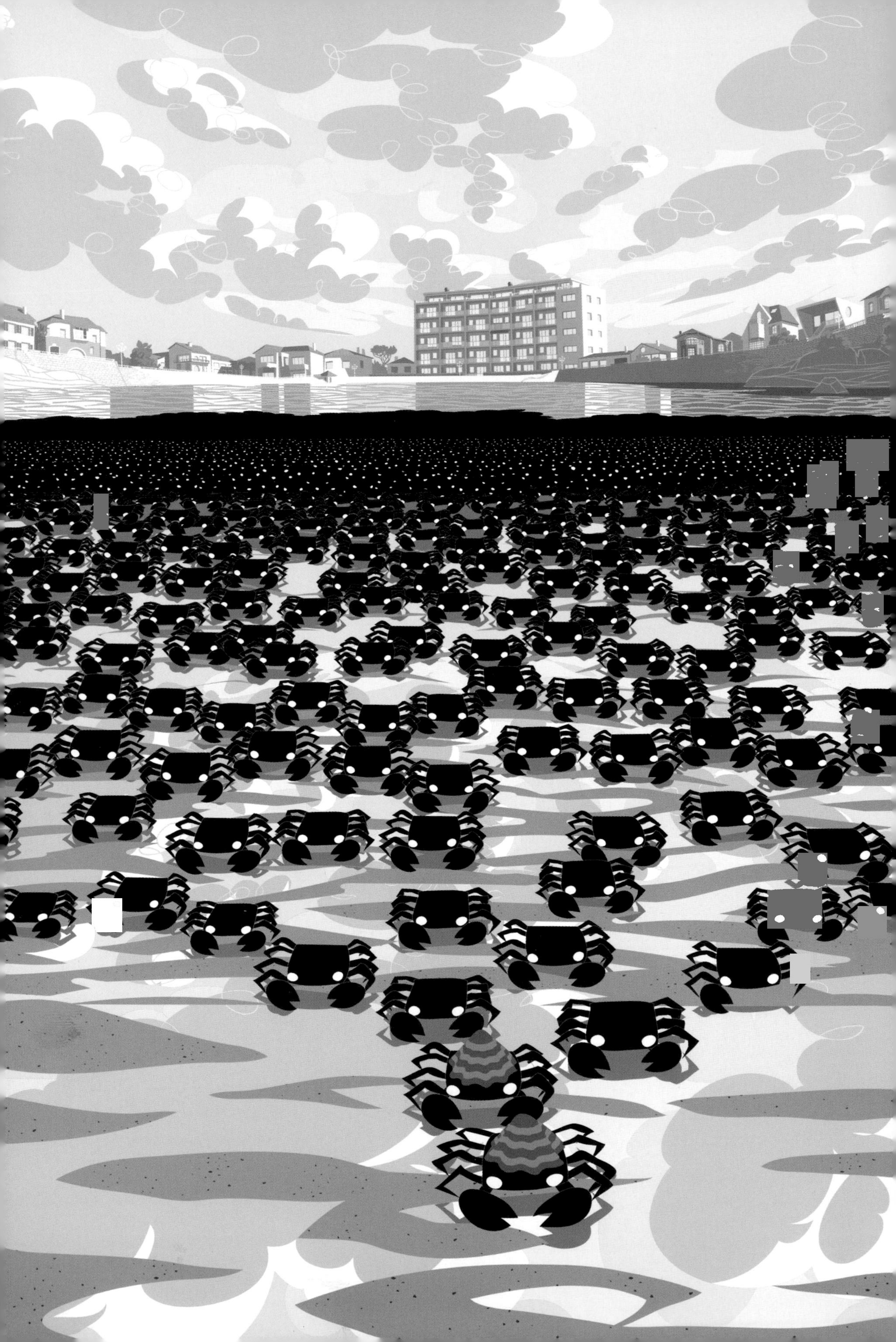

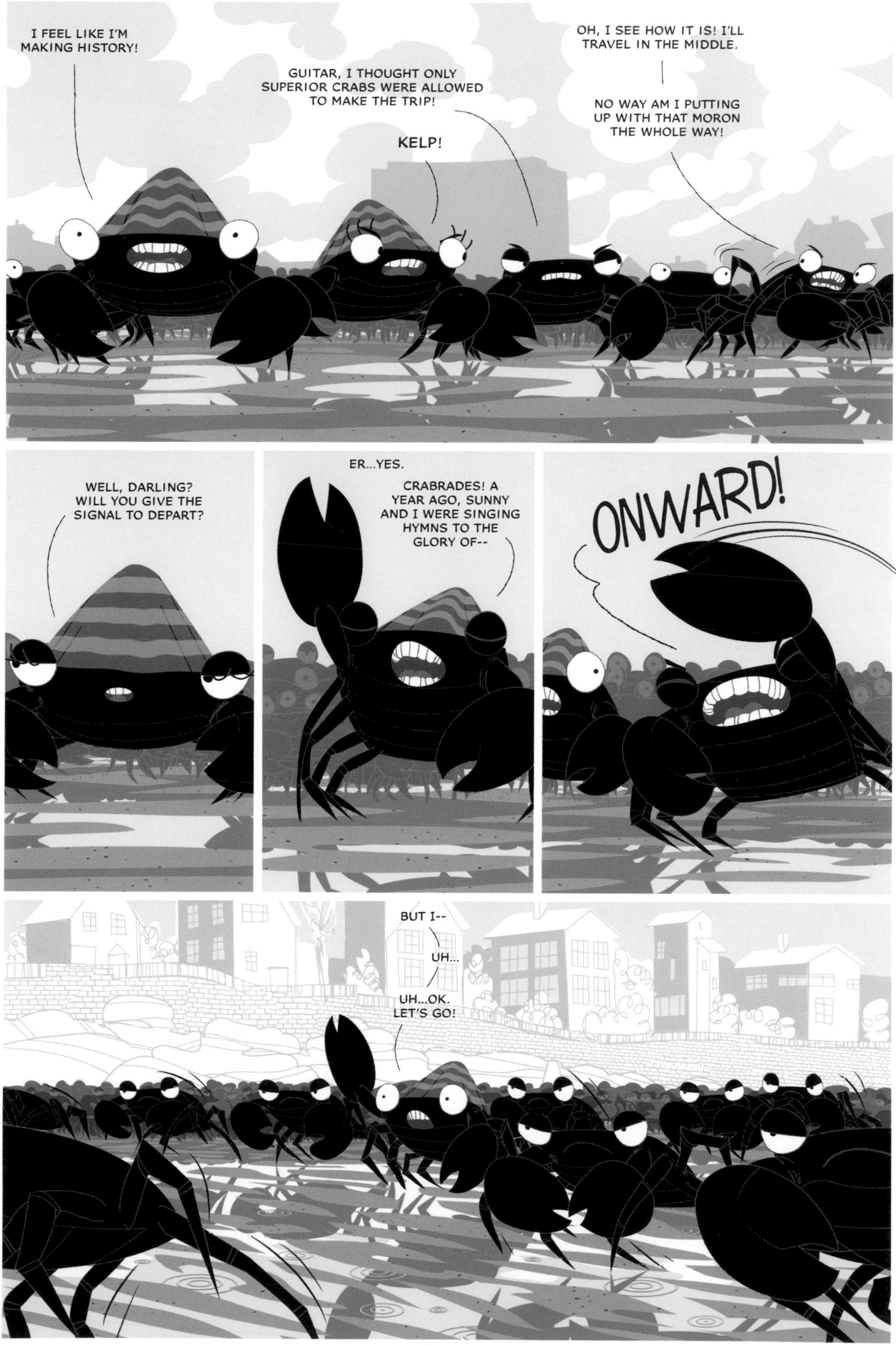

I FEEL LIKE I'M MAKING HISTORY!
GUITAR, I THOUGHT ONLY SUPERIOR CRABS WERE ALLOWED TO MAKE THE TRIP!
KELP!
OH, I SEE HOW IT IS! I'LL TRAVEL IN THE MIDDLE.
NO WAY AM I PUTTING UP WITH THAT MORON THE WHOLE WAY!
WELL, DARLING? WILL YOU GIVE THE SIGNAL TO DEPART?
ER...YES.
CRABRADES! A YEAR AGO, SUNNY AND I WERE SINGING HYMNS TO THE GLORY OF--
ONWARD!
BUT I--
UH...
UH...OK. LET'S GO!

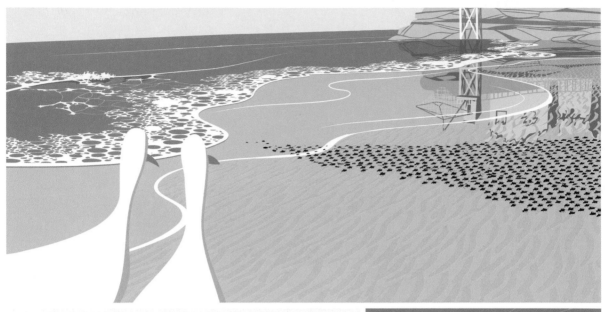

SO THEY'RE A MIGRATING SPECIES NOW!

I'M GOING TO MISS THEM.

WEIRD, ISN'T IT? NOW THAT THEY CAN EACH PICK THEIR OWN DIRECTION, THEY STILL WIND UP ALL HEADING THE SAME WAY.

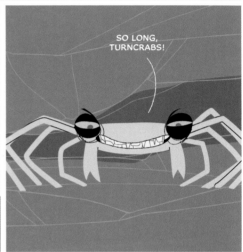

SO LONG, TURNCRABS!

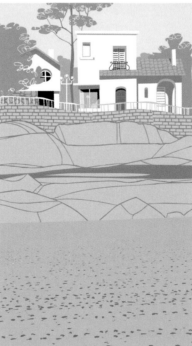

CHTOUNK!

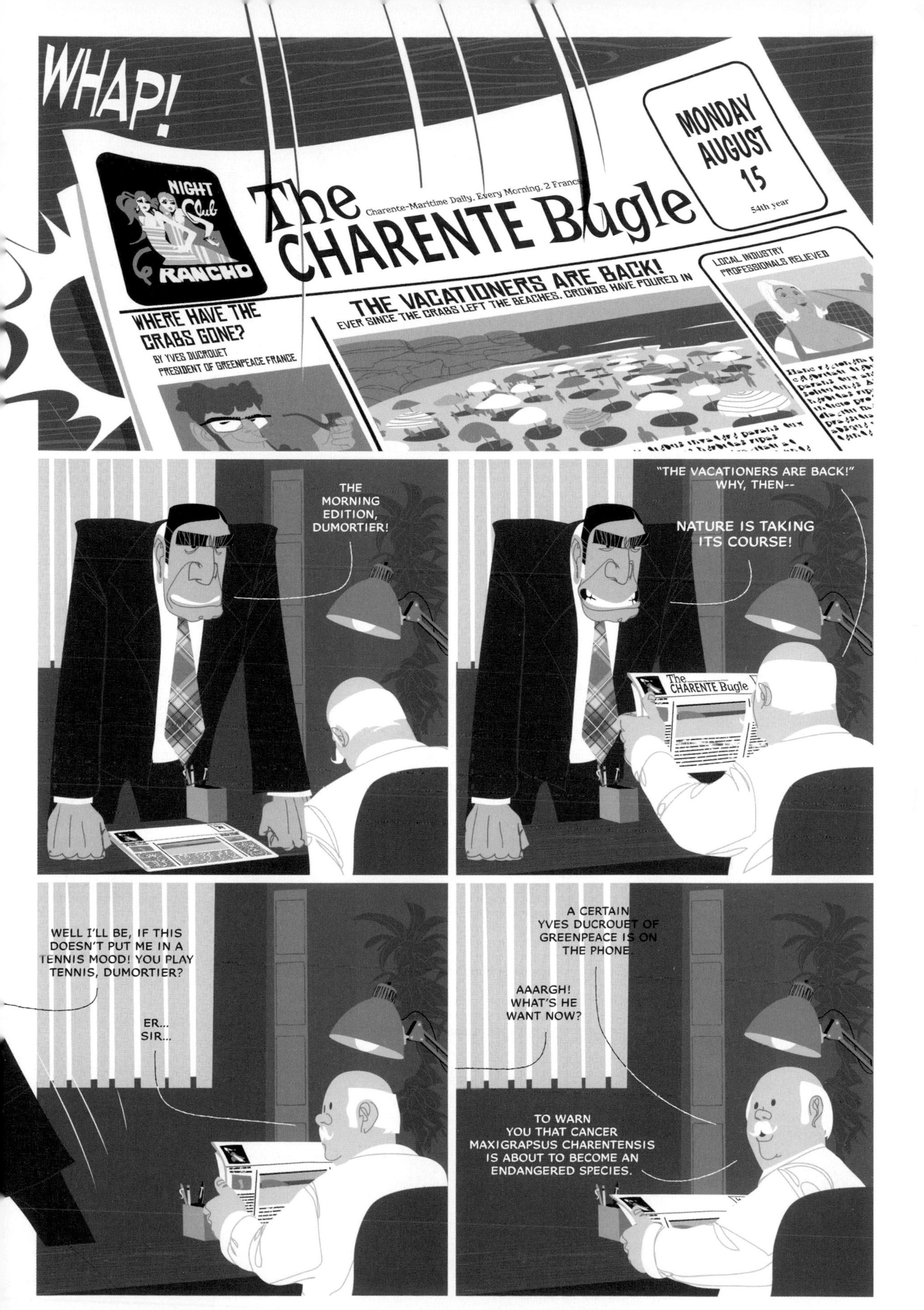
WHAP!
NIGHT Club RANCHO
The CHARENTE Bugle
Charente-Maritime Daily. Every Morning. 2 Francs
MONDAY AUGUST 15
54th year
WHERE HAVE THE CRABS GONE?
BY YVES DUCROUET
PRESIDENT OF GREENPEACE FRANCE
THE VACATIONERS ARE BACK!
EVER SINCE THE CRABS LEFT THE BEACHES, CROWDS HAVE POURED IN
LOCAL INDUSTRY PROFESSIONALS RELIEVED
THE MORNING EDITION, DUMORTIER!
"THE VACATIONERS ARE BACK!" WHY, THEN--
NATURE IS TAKING ITS COURSE!
The CHARENTE Bugle
WELL I'LL BE, IF THIS DOESN'T PUT ME IN A TENNIS MOOD! YOU PLAY TENNIS, DUMORTIER?
ER... SIR...
A CERTAIN YVES DUCROUET OF GREENPEACE IS ON THE PHONE.
AAARGH! WHAT'S HE WANT NOW?
TO WARN YOU THAT CANCER MAXIGRAPSUS CHARENTENSIS IS ABOUT TO BECOME AN ENDANGERED SPECIES.

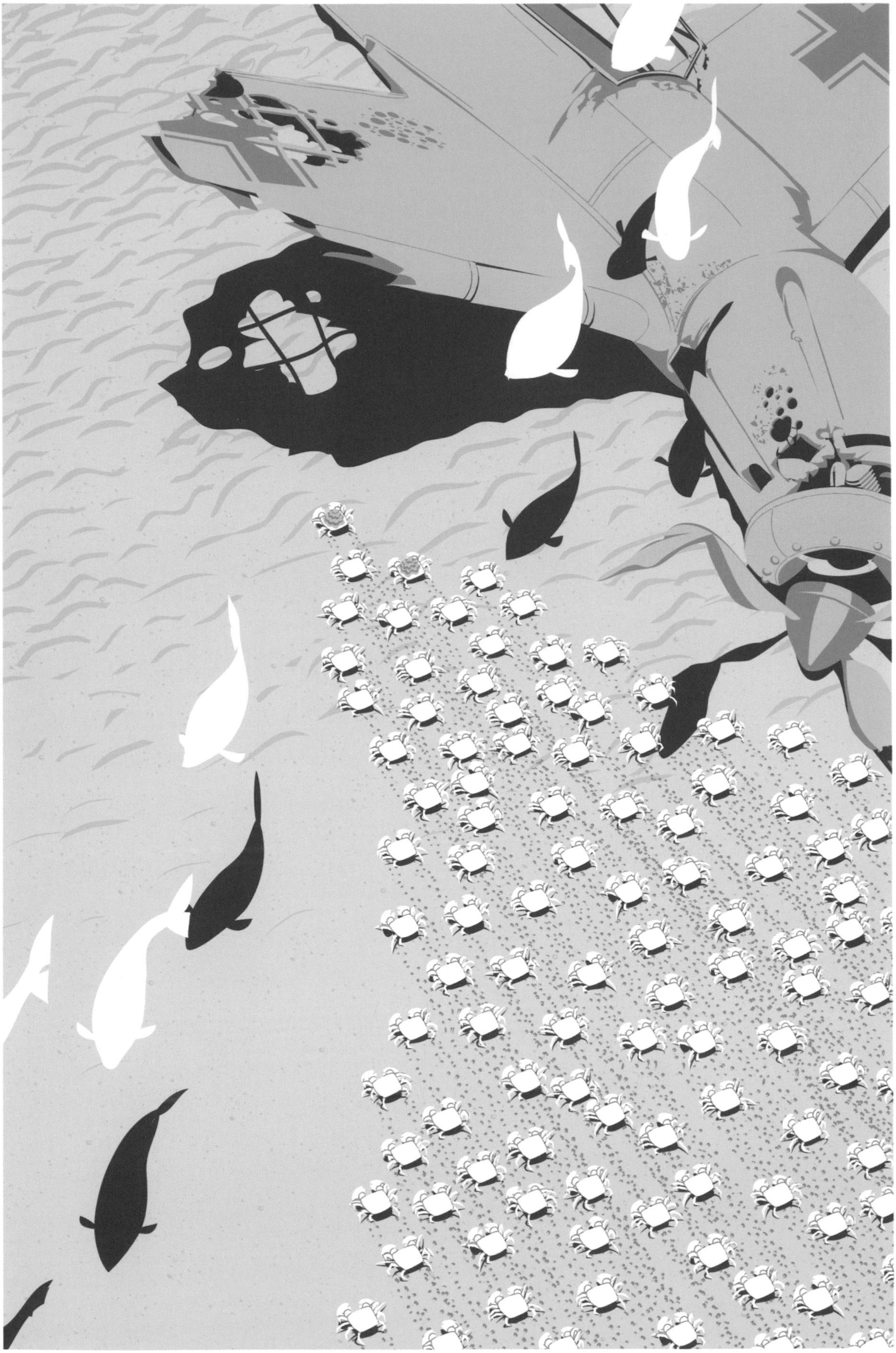

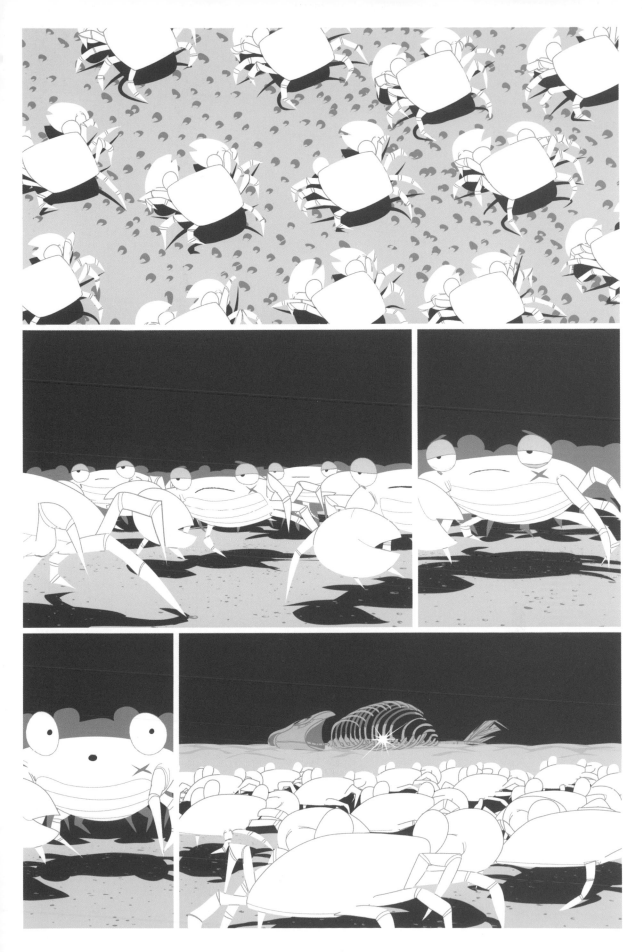

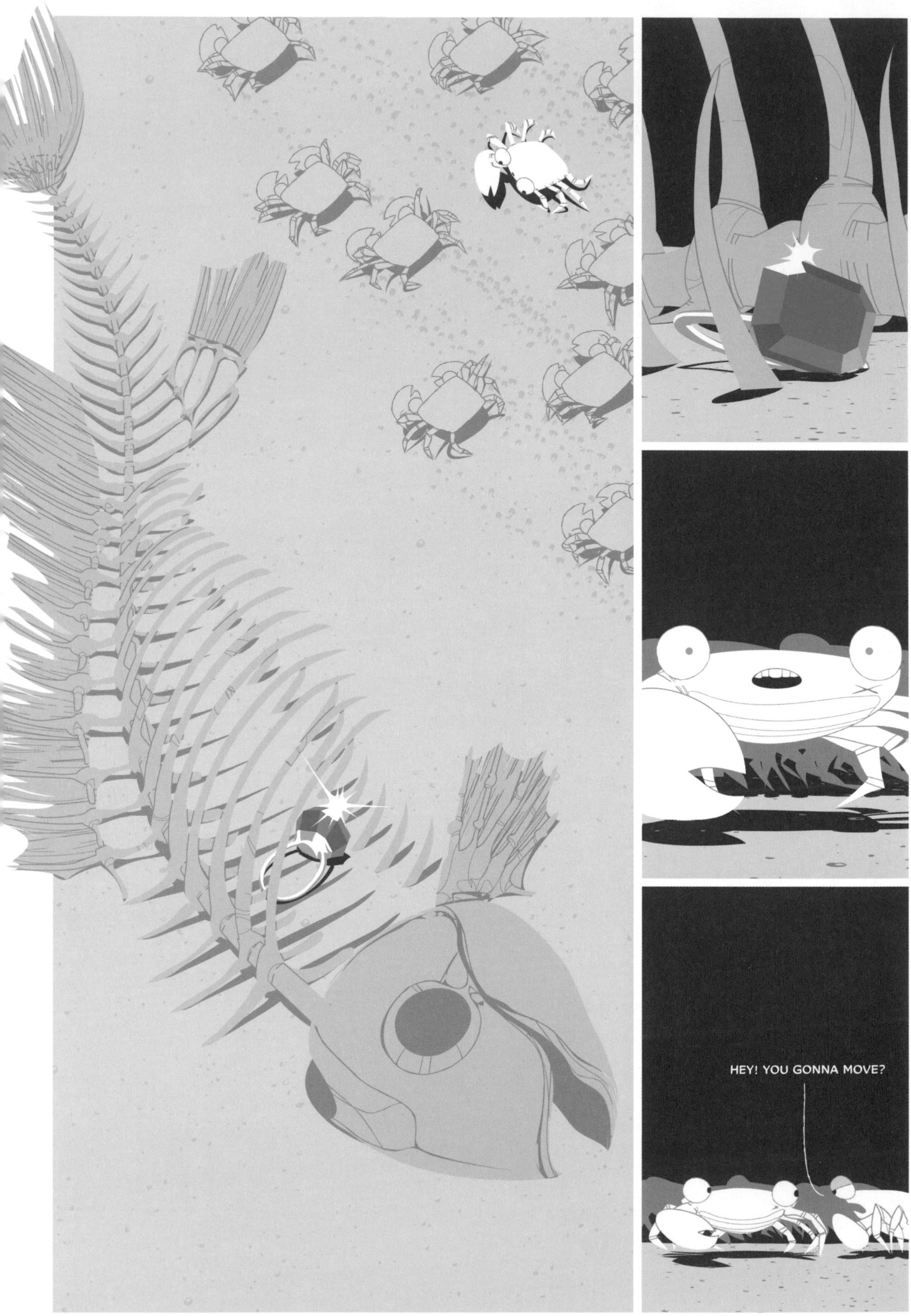
HEY! YOU GONNA MOVE?

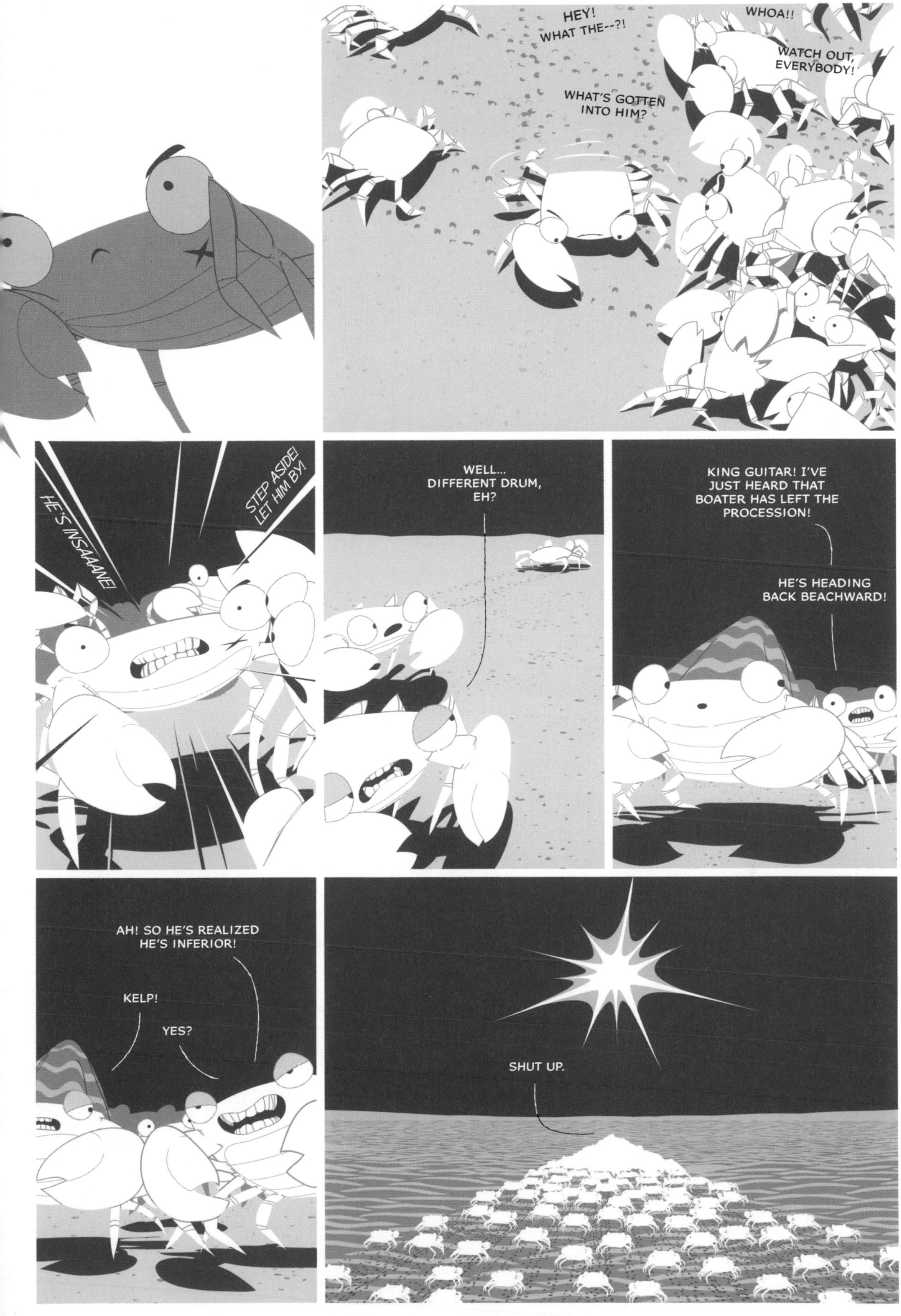
HEY!
WHAT THE--?!
WHOA!!
WATCH OUT, EVERYBODY!
WHAT'S GOTTEN INTO HIM?
HE'S INSAAANE!
STEP ASIDE! LET HIM BY!
WELL... DIFFERENT DRUM, EH?
KING GUITAR! I'VE JUST HEARD THAT BOATER HAS LEFT THE PROCESSION!
HE'S HEADING BACK BEACHWARD!
AH! SO HE'S REALIZED HE'S INFERIOR!
KELP!
YES?
SHUT UP.

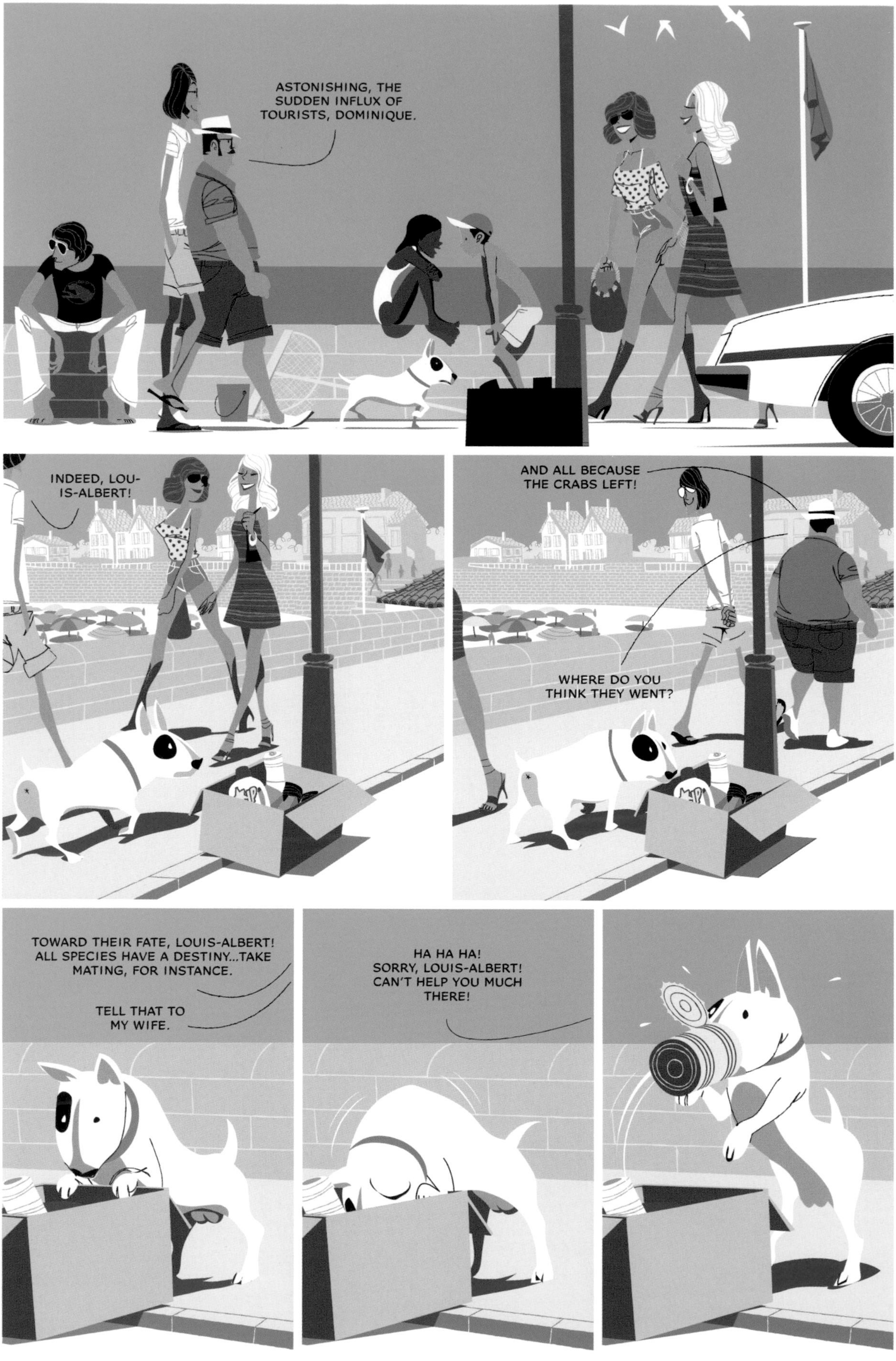
ASTONISHING, THE SUDDEN INFLUX OF TOURISTS, DOMINIQUE.
INDEED, LOU-IS-ALBERT!
AND ALL BECAUSE THE CRABS LEFT!
WHERE DO YOU THINK THEY WENT?
TOWARD THEIR FATE, LOUIS-ALBERT! ALL SPECIES HAVE A DESTINY...TAKE MATING, FOR INSTANCE.
TELL THAT TO MY WIFE.
HA HA HA! SORRY, LOUIS-ALBERT! CAN'T HELP YOU MUCH THERE!

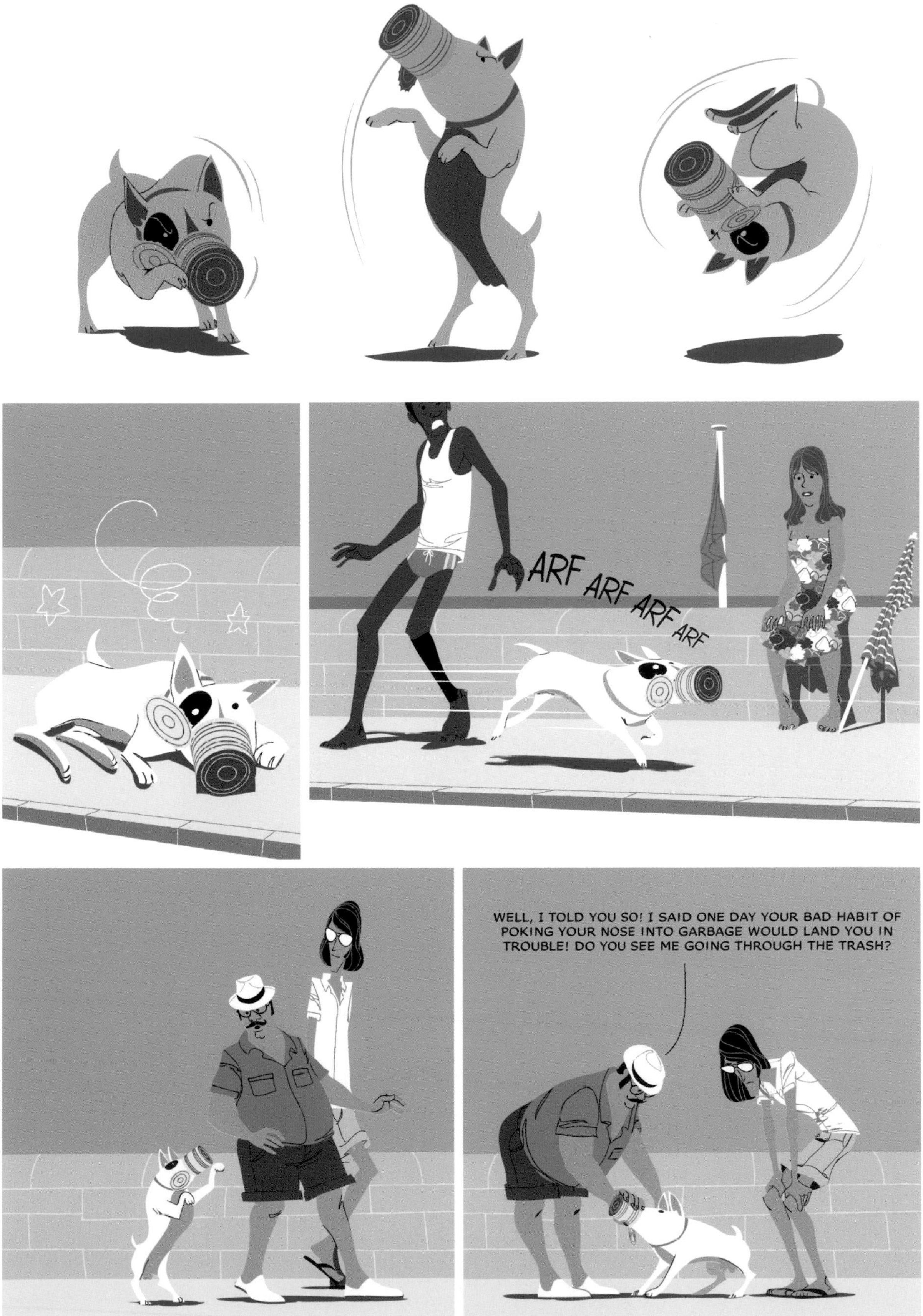
ARF ARF ARF ARF
WELL, I TOLD YOU SO! I SAID ONE DAY YOUR BAD HABIT OF POKING YOUR NOSE INTO GARBAGE WOULD LAND YOU IN TROUBLE! DO YOU SEE ME GOING THROUGH THE TRASH?

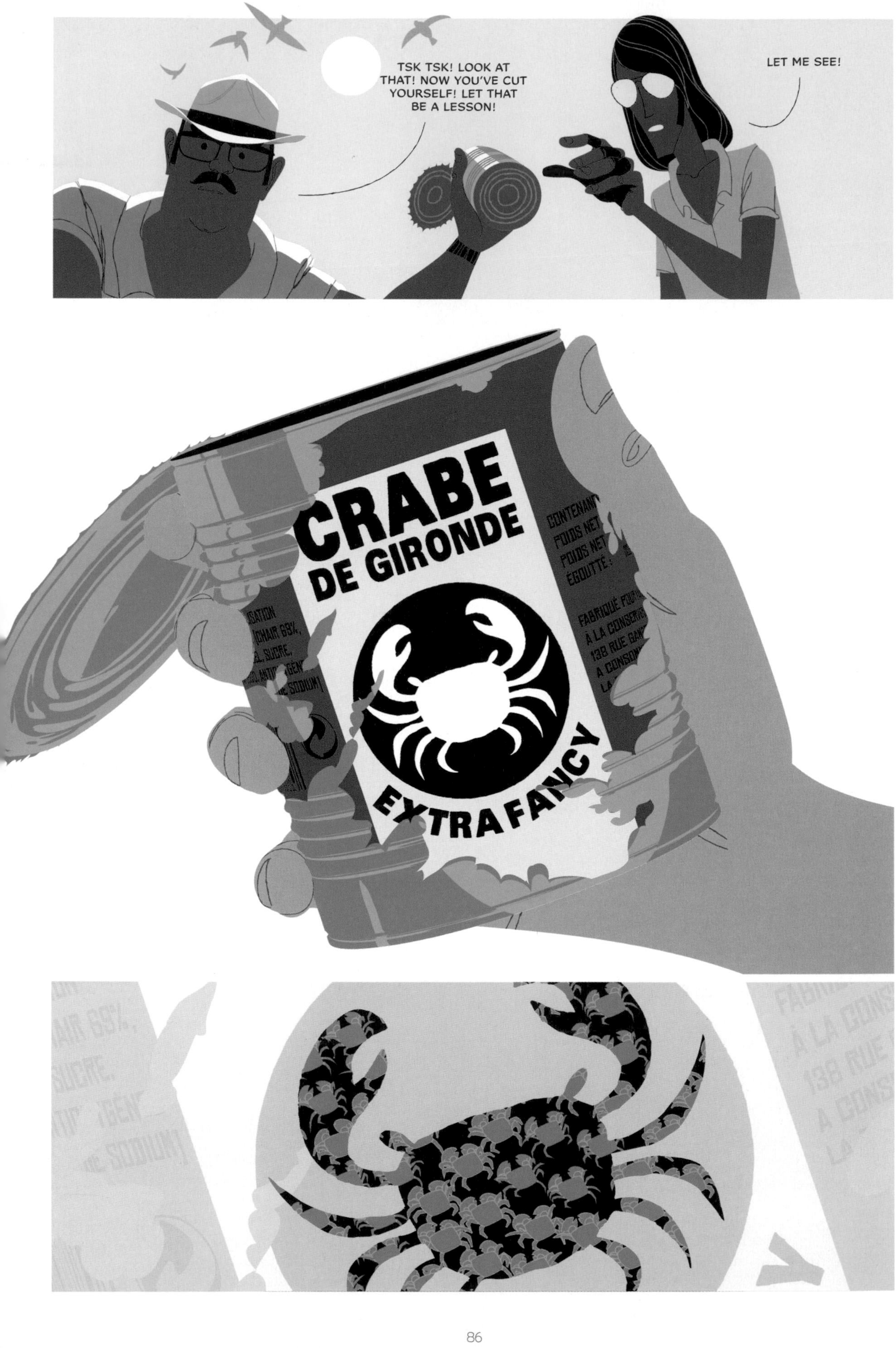
TSK TSK! LOOK AT THAT! NOW YOU'VE CUT YOURSELF! LET THAT BE A LESSON!
LET ME SEE!
CRABE
DE GIRONDE
EXTRA FANCY
POIDS NET
ÉGOUTTÉ :

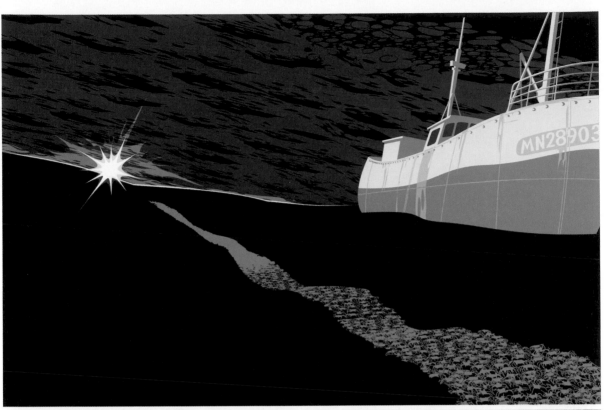

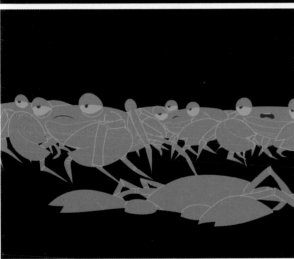

WE'LL SURE HAVE EARNED OUR EVOLUTION, WON'T WE, KELP?

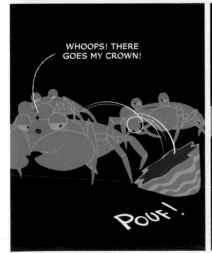

WHOOPS! THERE GOES MY CROWN!

POUF!

KELP! IF YOU'VE BEEN TELLING TALL TALES, I'LL--

SEE? I WASN'T LYING! GUITAR, GET A LOAD OF THIS!

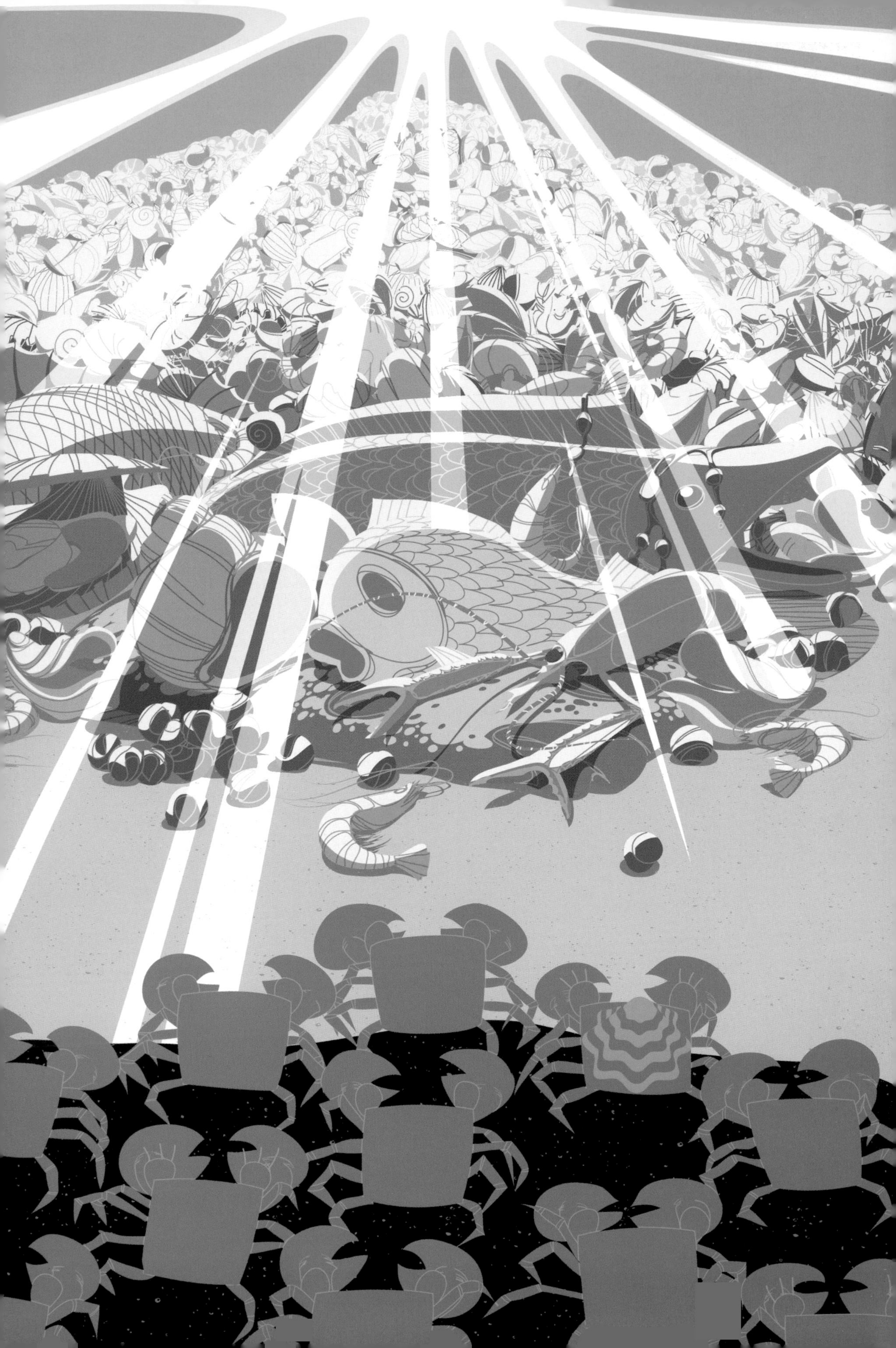

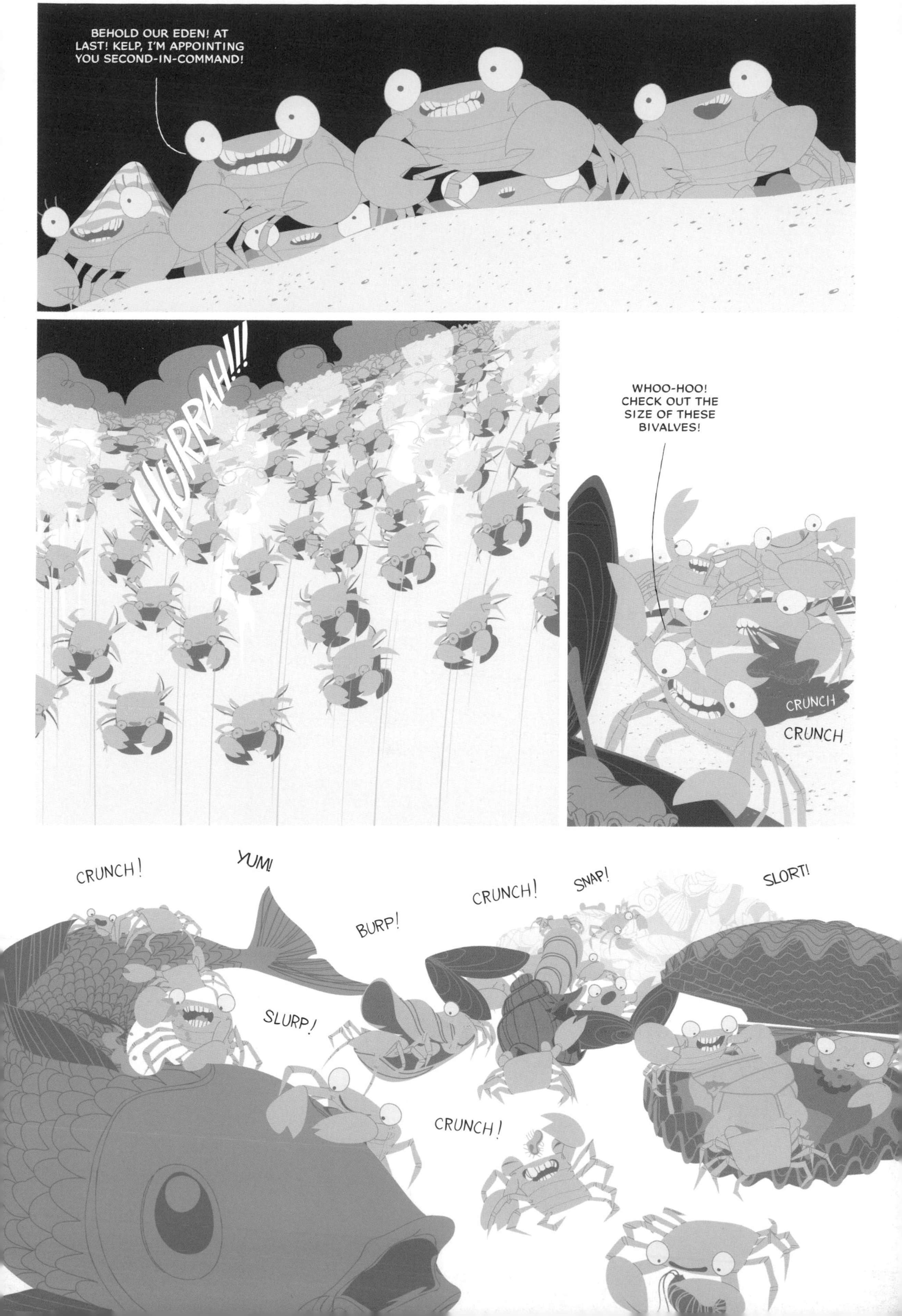
BEHOLD OUR EDEN! AT LAST! KELP, I'M APPOINTING YOU SECOND-IN-COMMAND!
HURRAH!!!
WHOO-HOO! CHECK OUT THE SIZE OF THESE BIVALVES!
CRUNCH
CRUNCH
CRUNCH!
YUM!
CRUNCH!
SNAP!
SLORT!
BURP!
SLURP!
CRUNCH!

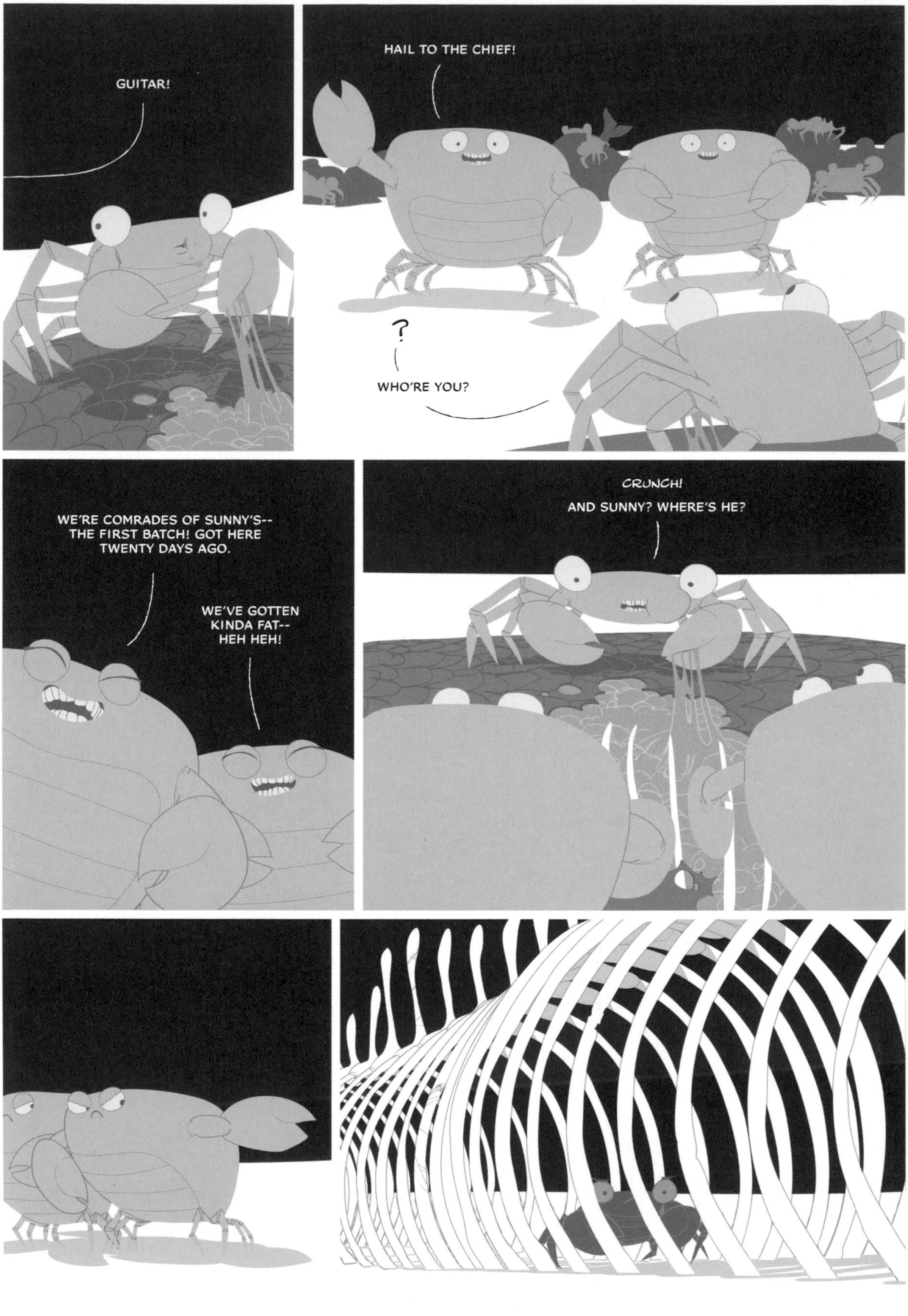
GUITAR!
HAIL TO THE CHIEF!
?
WHO'RE YOU?
WE'RE COMRADES OF SUNNY'S-- THE FIRST BATCH! GOT HERE TWENTY DAYS AGO.
WE'VE GOTTEN KINDA FAT-- HEH HEH!
CRUNCH!
AND SUNNY? WHERE'S HE?

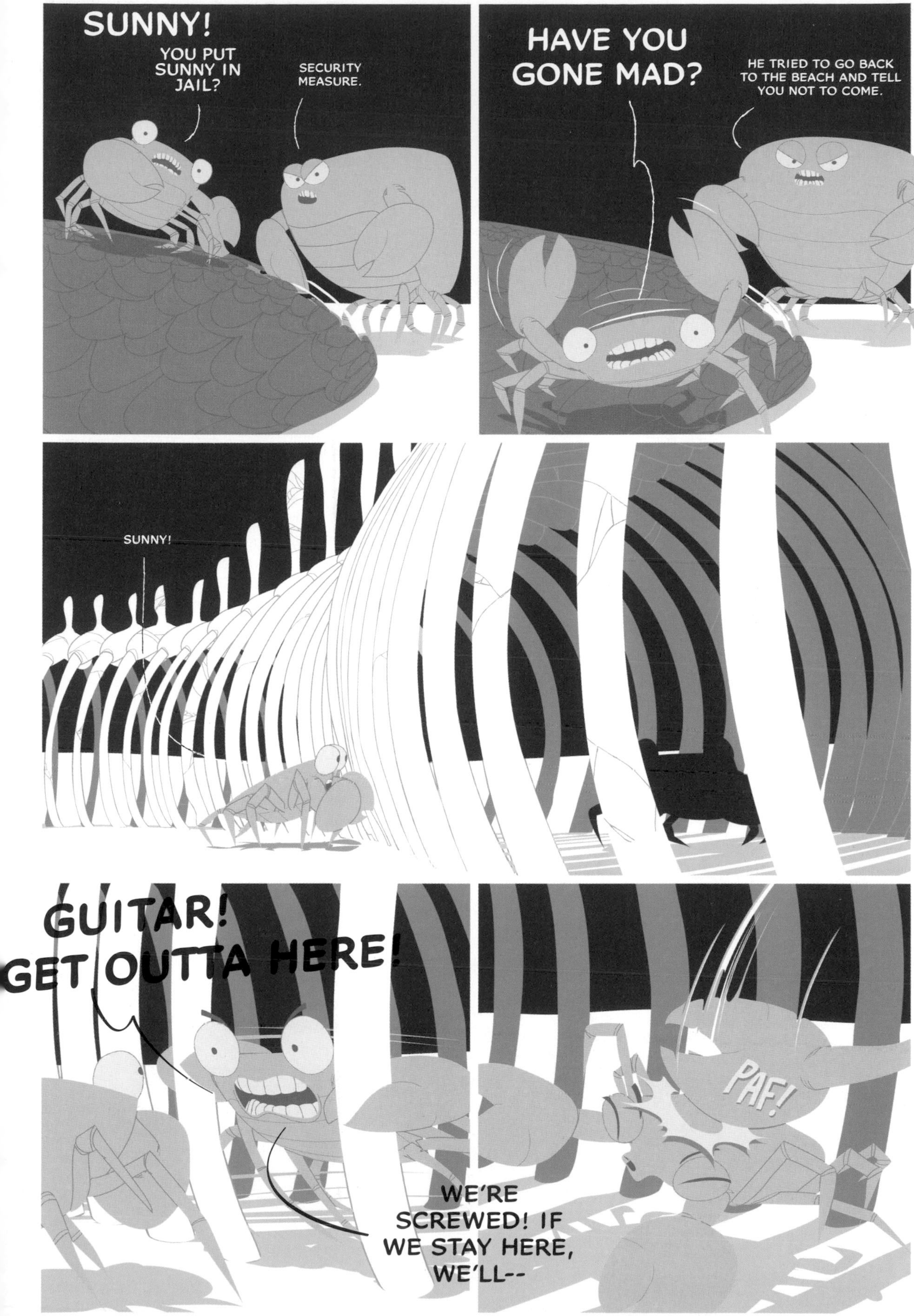
SUNNY!
YOU PUT SUNNY IN JAIL?
SECURITY MEASURE.
HAVE YOU GONE MAD?
HE TRIED TO GO BACK TO THE BEACH AND TELL YOU NOT TO COME.
SUNNY!
GUITAR! GET OUTTA HERE!
WE'RE SCREWED! IF WE STAY HERE, WE'LL--
PAF!

HEY!
WHY'D YOU KNOCK
HIM OUT?
THAT TRAITOR WANTS TO
CONVINCE US TO LEAVE THIS PLACE.
HE WANTS TO GIVE
UP ON EVOLUTION.
HE SAYS WE'VE
TAKEN IT TOO FAR.
SUNNY?
OUR GUIDE?
HE'S BACK-
SCUTTLING?
HMM...
GOOD WORK, FELLAS!
WE'LL KEEP AN EYE
ON HIM, CHIEF!

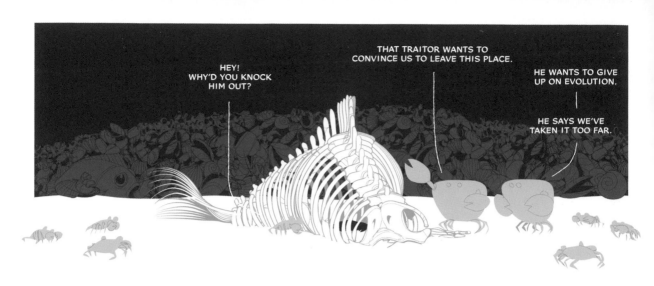

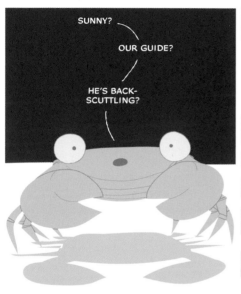

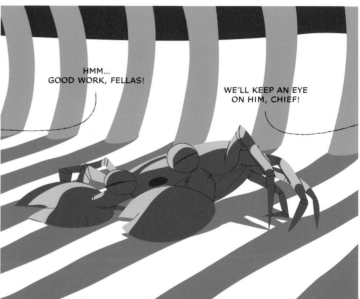

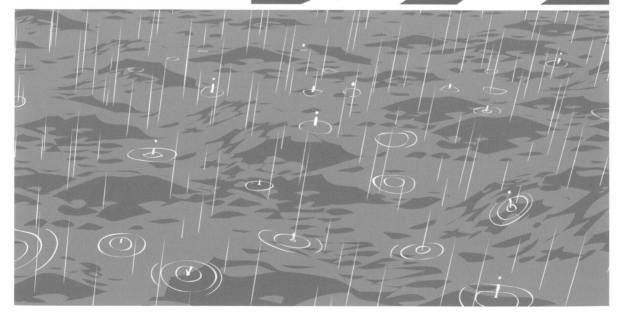

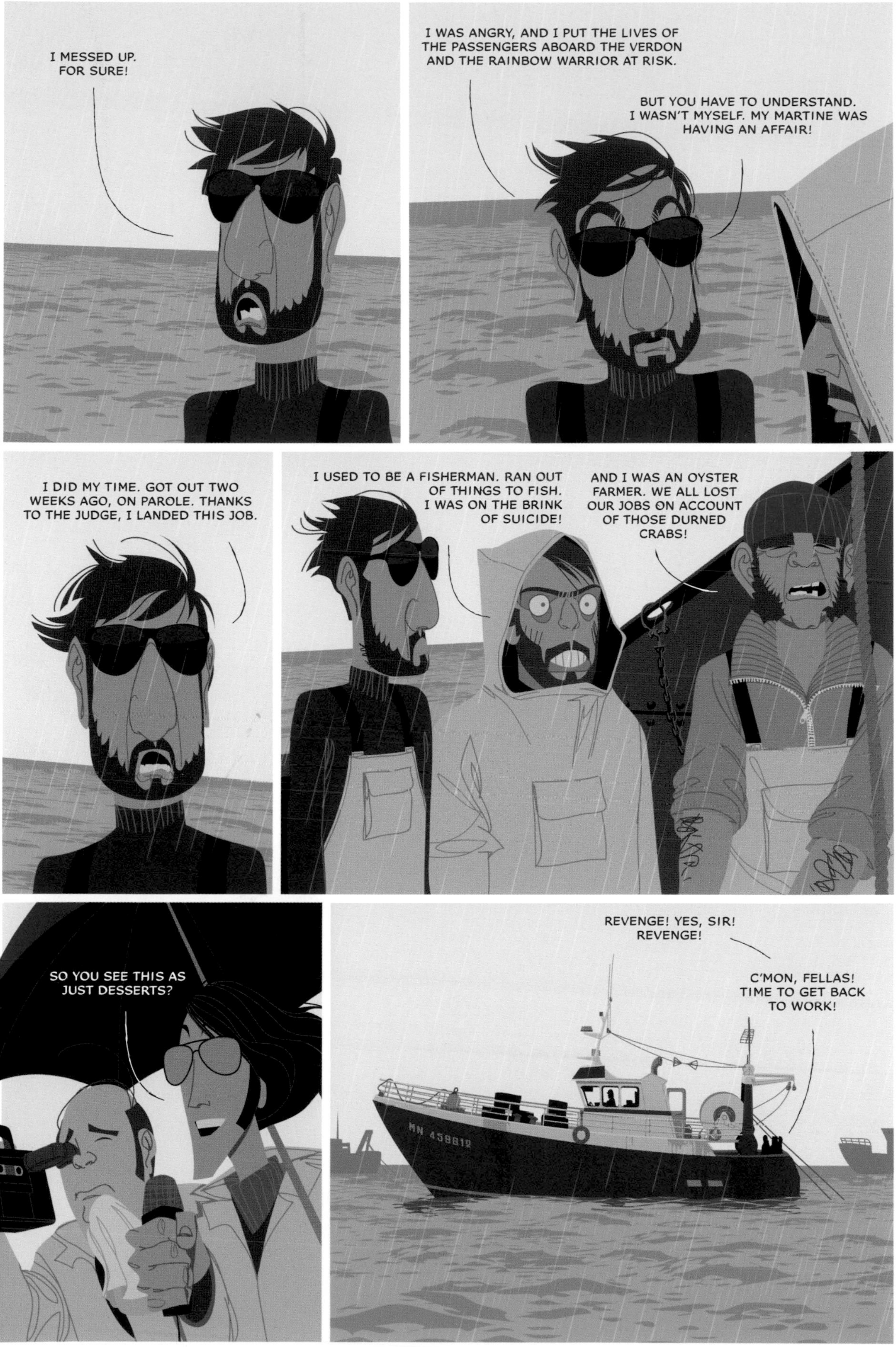
I MESSED UP. FOR SURE!
I WAS ANGRY, AND I PUT THE LIVES OF THE PASSENGERS ABOARD THE VERDON AND THE RAINBOW WARRIOR AT RISK.
BUT YOU HAVE TO UNDERSTAND. I WASN'T MYSELF. MY MARTINE WAS HAVING AN AFFAIR!
I DID MY TIME. GOT OUT TWO WEEKS AGO, ON PAROLE. THANKS TO THE JUDGE, I LANDED THIS JOB.
I USED TO BE A FISHERMAN. RAN OUT OF THINGS TO FISH. I WAS ON THE BRINK OF SUICIDE!
AND I WAS AN OYSTER FARMER. WE ALL LOST OUR JOBS ON ACCOUNT OF THOSE DURNED CRABS!
SO YOU SEE THIS AS JUST DESSERTS?
REVENGE! YES, SIR! REVENGE!
C'MON, FELLAS! TIME TO GET BACK TO WORK!
MN 459812

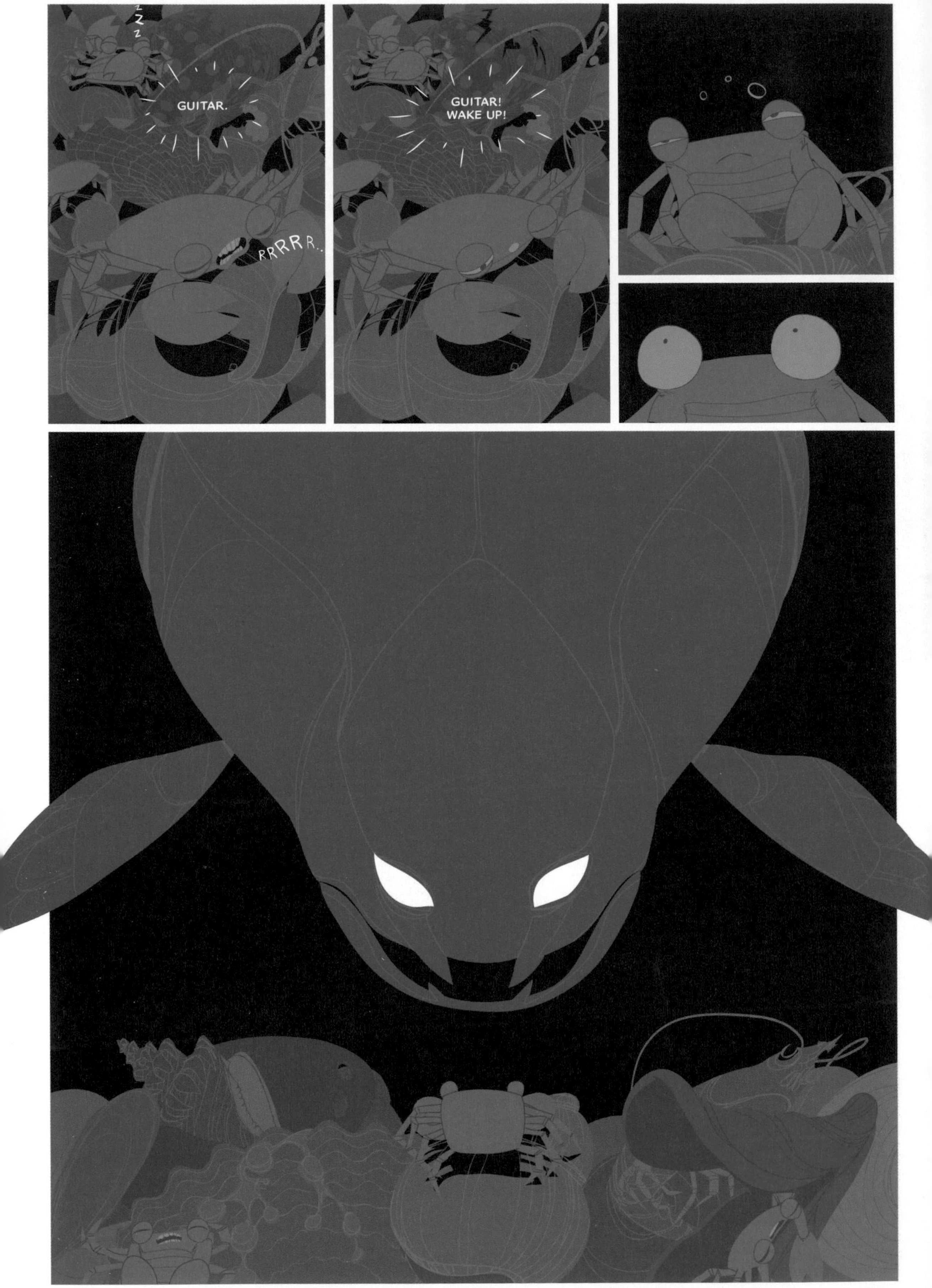
Z Z Z
GUITAR.
RRRRR..
GUITAR! WAKE UP!

AAAAmmmh...

CALM DOWN, GUITAR. IT'S ME, SUNNY.

SCREAM, AND MY FRIEND ACHILLES WILL EAT YOU. GOT IT?

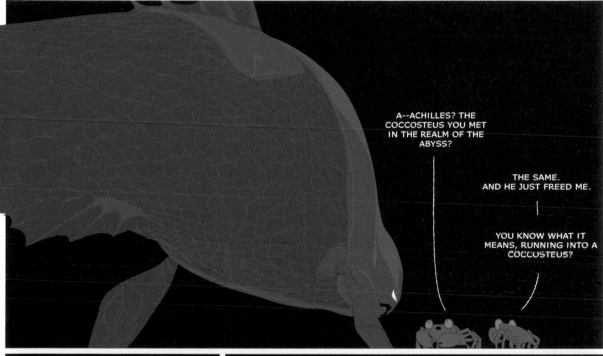

A--ACHILLES? THE COCCOSTEUS YOU MET IN THE REALM OF THE ABYSS?

THE SAME. AND HE JUST FREED ME.

YOU KNOW WHAT IT MEANS, RUNNING INTO A COCCOSTEUS?

IT MEANS YOU'RE IN DEEP. WAAAAY DEEP DOWN.

NOW, COME WITH ME.

WE--WE'RE GETTING ON THE BACK OF THAT MONSTER?

YES.

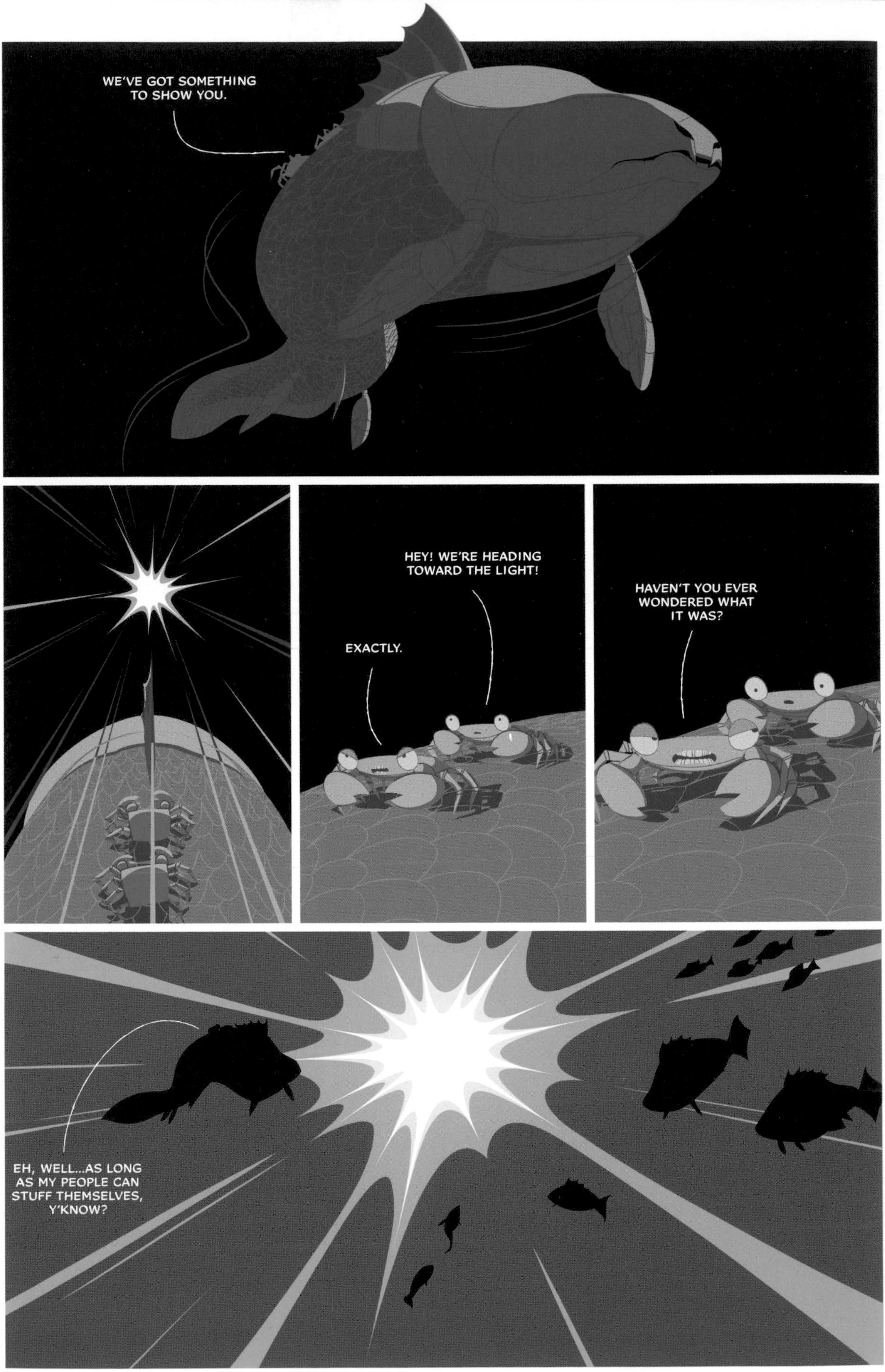
WE'VE GOT SOMETHING TO SHOW YOU.
HEY! WE'RE HEADING TOWARD THE LIGHT!
EXACTLY.
HAVEN'T YOU EVER WONDERED WHAT IT WAS?
EH, WELL...AS LONG AS MY PEOPLE CAN STUFF THEMSELVES, Y'KNOW?

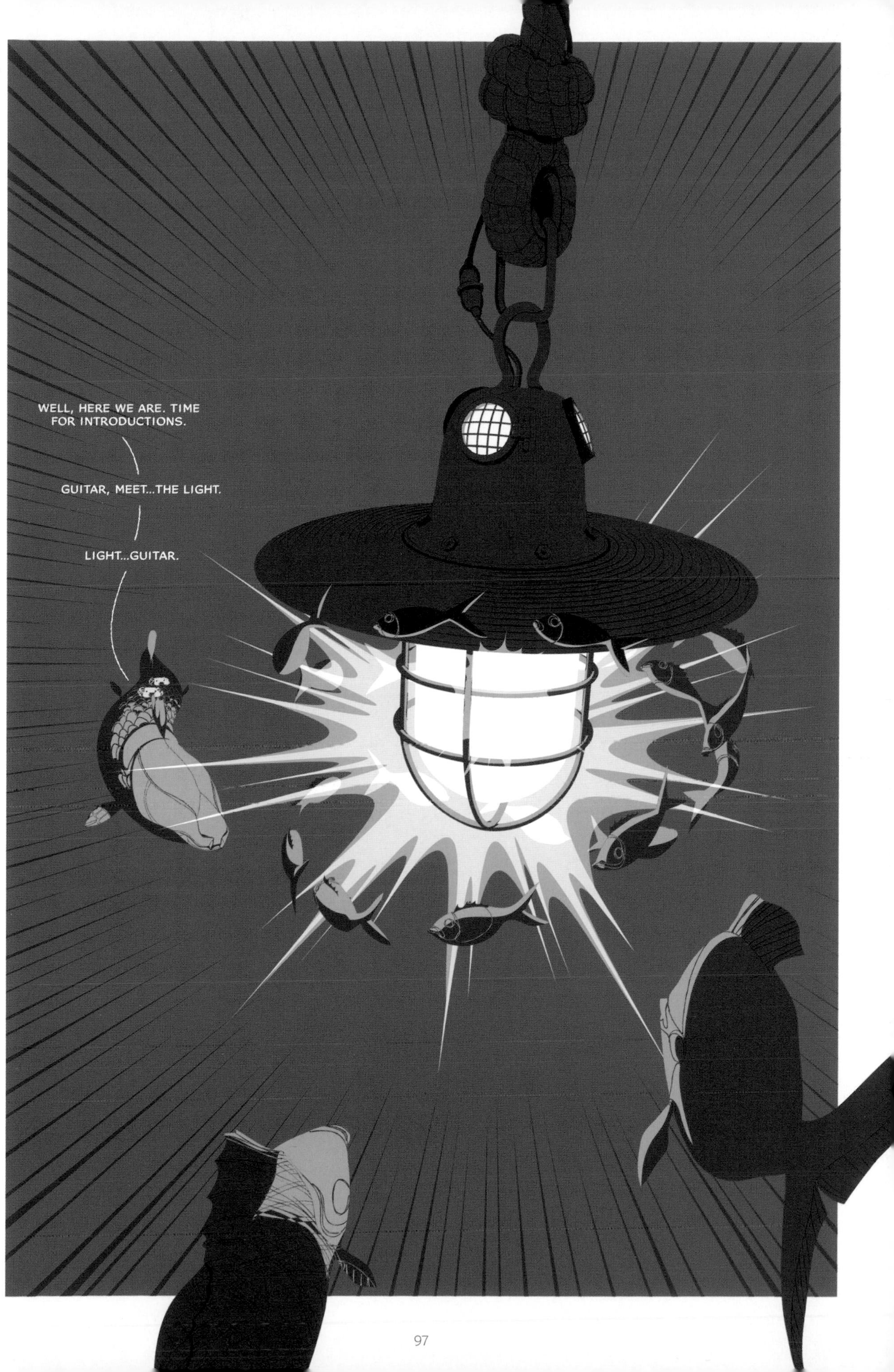
WELL, HERE WE ARE. TIME FOR INTRODUCTIONS.
GUITAR, MEET...THE LIGHT.
LIGHT...GUITAR.

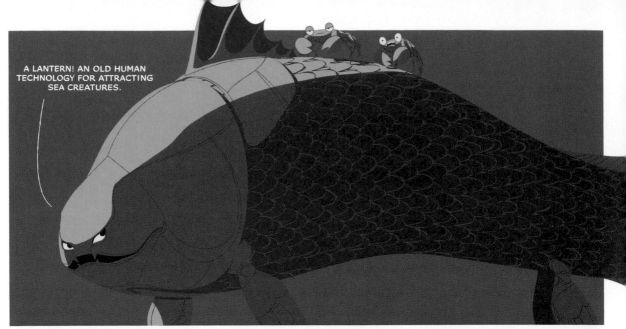

A LANTERN! AN OLD HUMAN TECHNOLOGY FOR ATTRACTING SEA CREATURES.

...

AAAH! WE GOT HAD! QUICK! EVERYBODY RUN!

GUITAR...

TOO LATE!

THE PRESSURE HERE IS SO GREAT THAT OUR KIND CAN NO LONGER GET BACK TO THE SURFACE. ESPECIALLY NOW THAT THEY'VE PUT ON WEIGHT.

BESIDES...

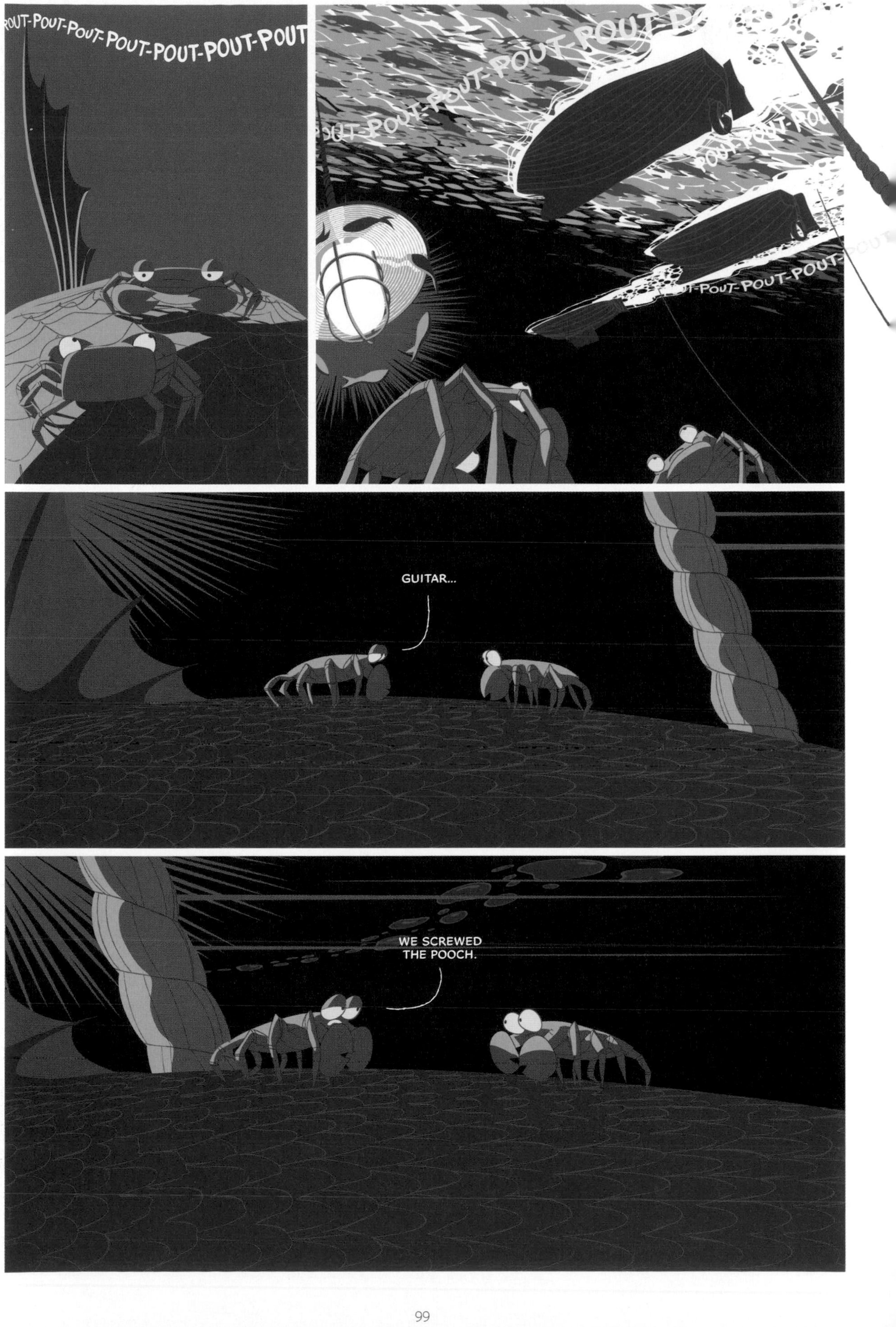
OUT-POUT-POUT-POUT-POUT-POUT
POUT-POUT-POUT-POUT
POUT-POUT-POUT
POUT-POUT-POUT-POUT
GUITAR...
WE SCREWED THE POOCH.

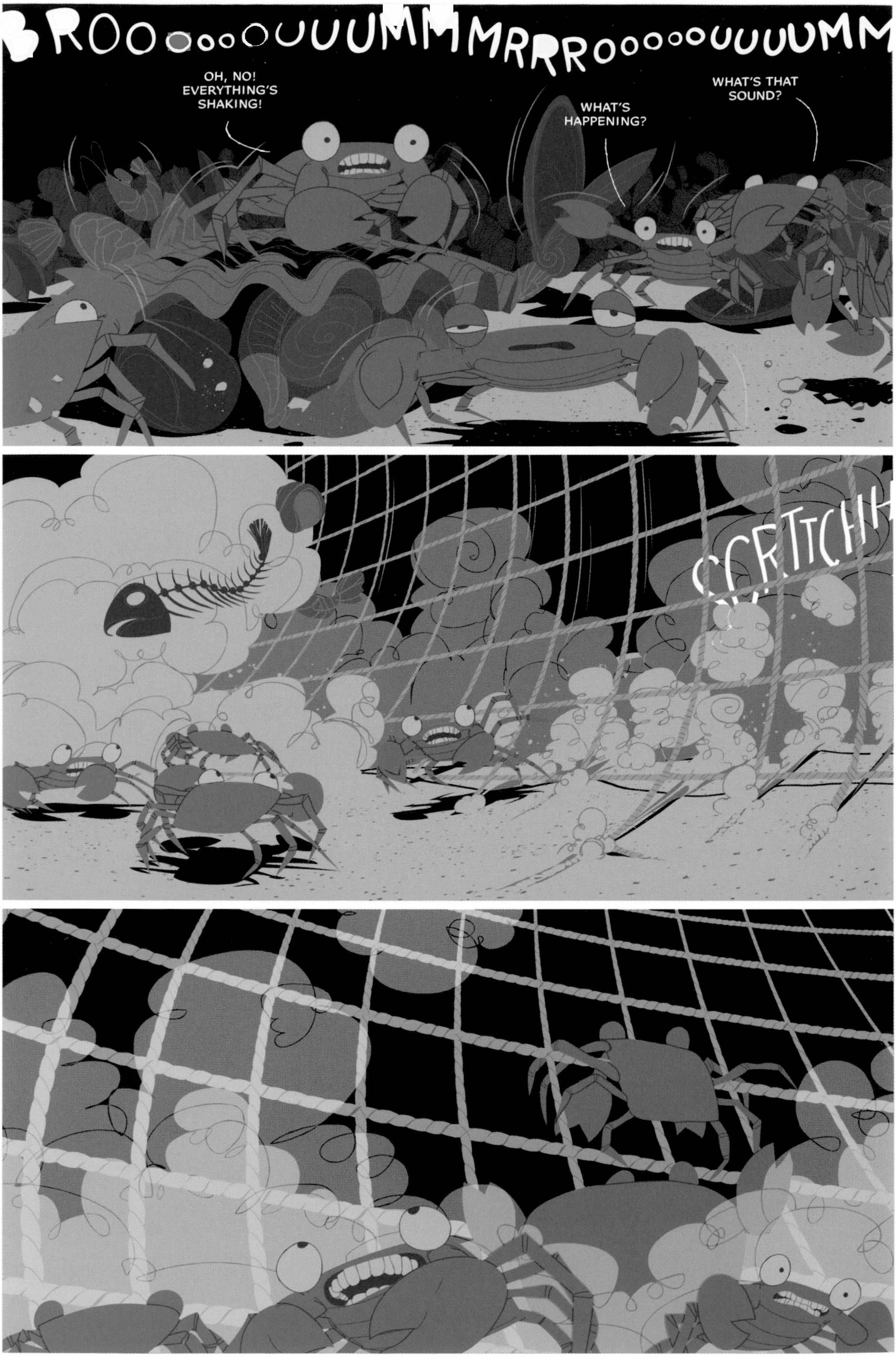
BROOoooOUUUUMMMRRROooooUUUUMM
OH, NO! EVERYTHING'S SHAKING!
WHAT'S HAPPENING?
WHAT'S THAT SOUND?
SCRTTCHH

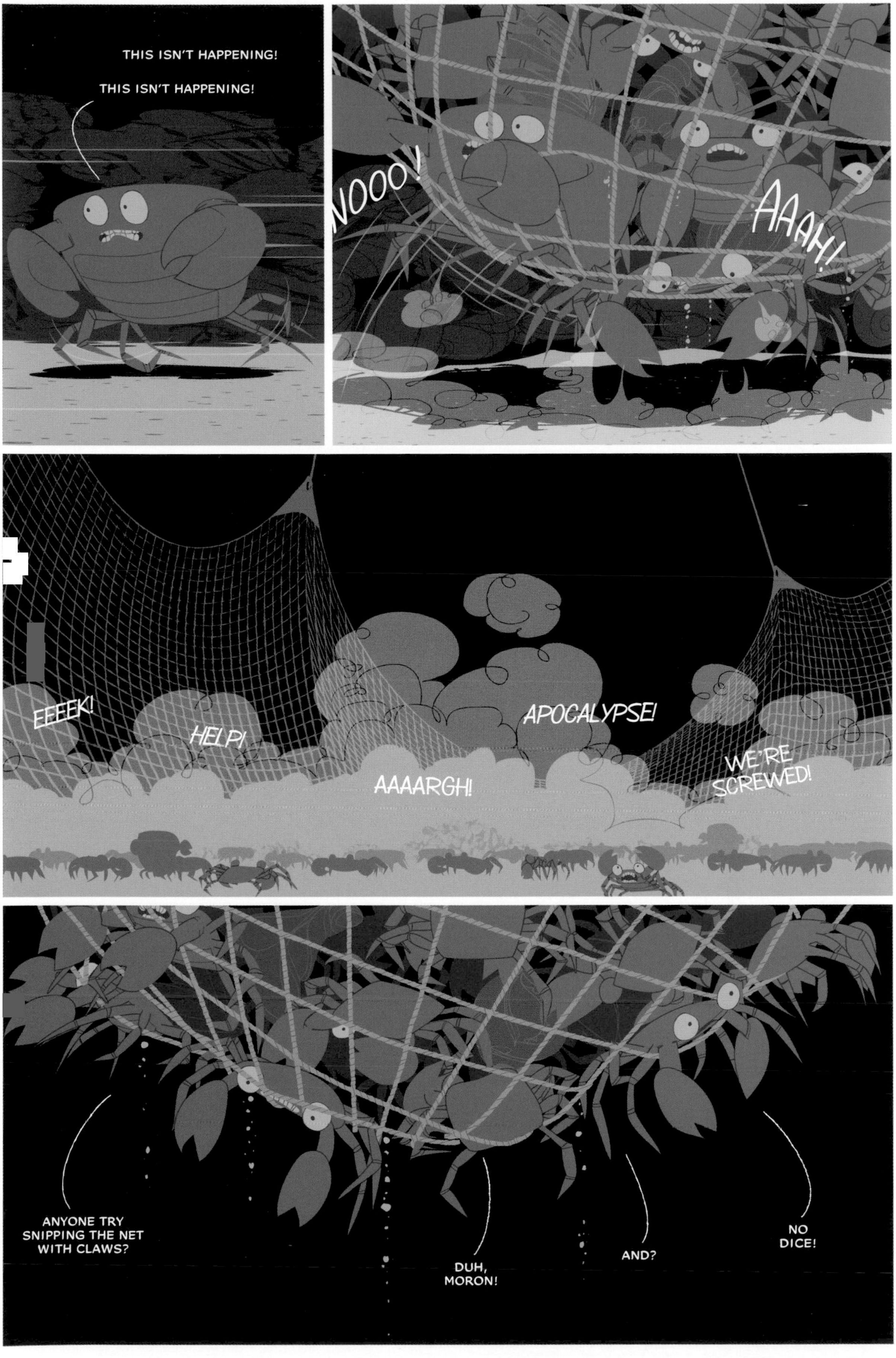
THIS ISN'T HAPPENING!
THIS ISN'T HAPPENING!
NOOO!
AAAH!
EEEEK!
HELP!
AAAARGH!
APOCALYPSE!
WE'RE SCREWED!
ANYONE TRY SNIPPING THE NET WITH CLAWS?
DUH, MORON!
AND?
NO DICE!

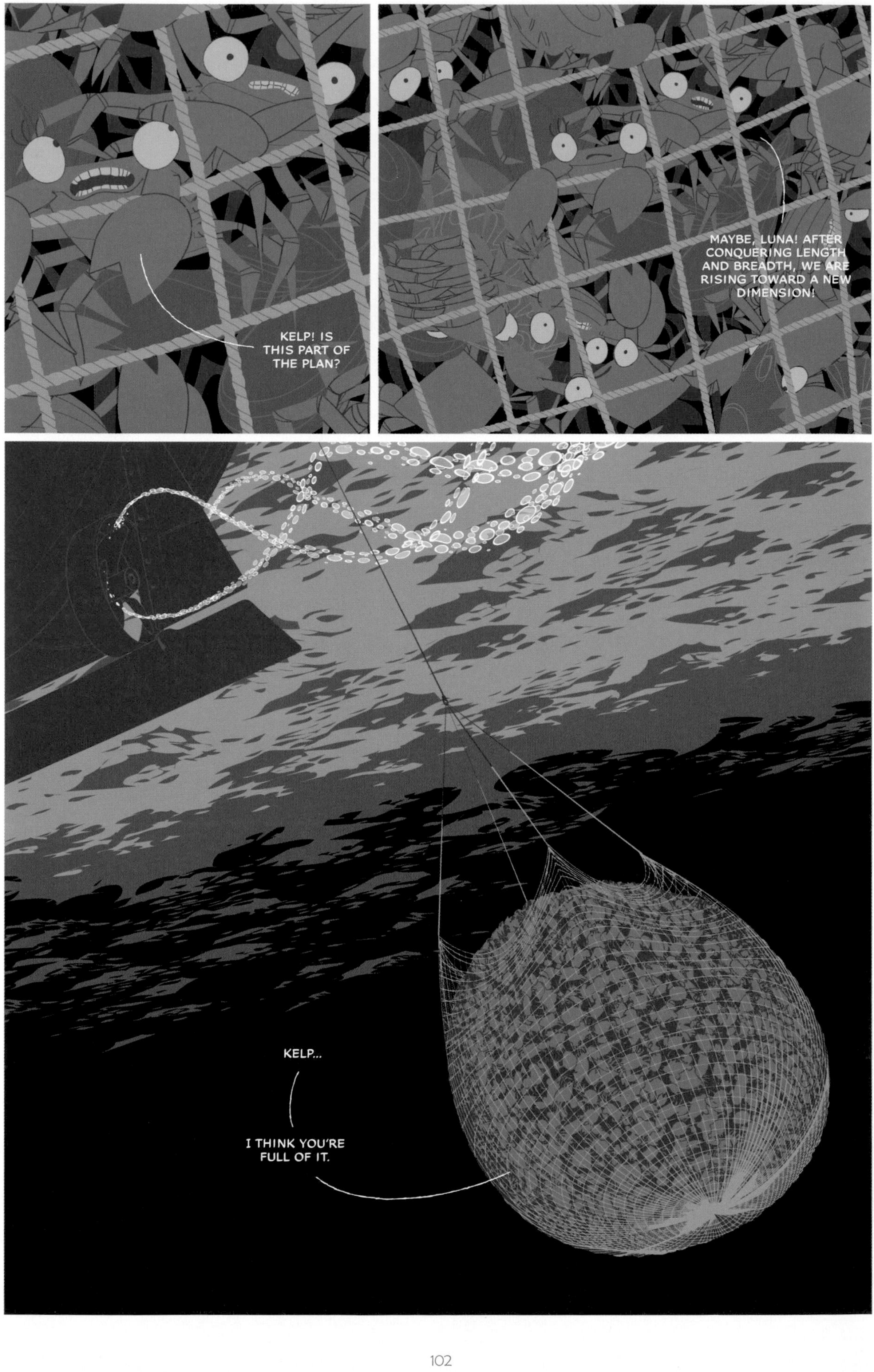
KELP! IS THIS PART OF THE PLAN?
MAYBE, LUNA! AFTER CONQUERING LENGTH AND BREADTH, WE ARE RISING TOWARD A NEW DIMENSION!
KELP...
I THINK YOU'RE FULL OF IT.

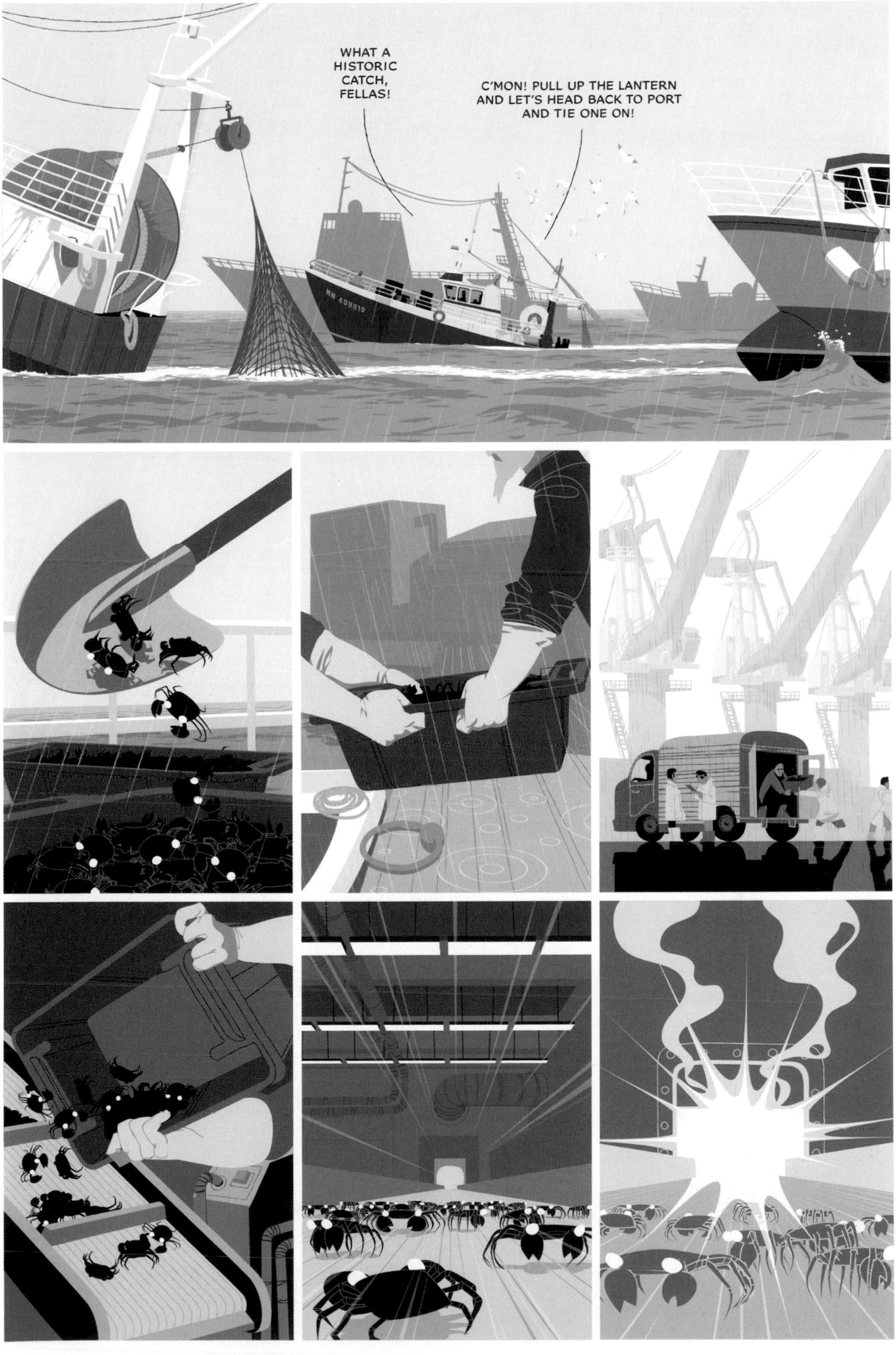
WHAT A HISTORIC CATCH, FELLAS!
C'MON! PULL UP THE LANTERN AND LET'S HEAD BACK TO PORT AND TIE ONE ON!

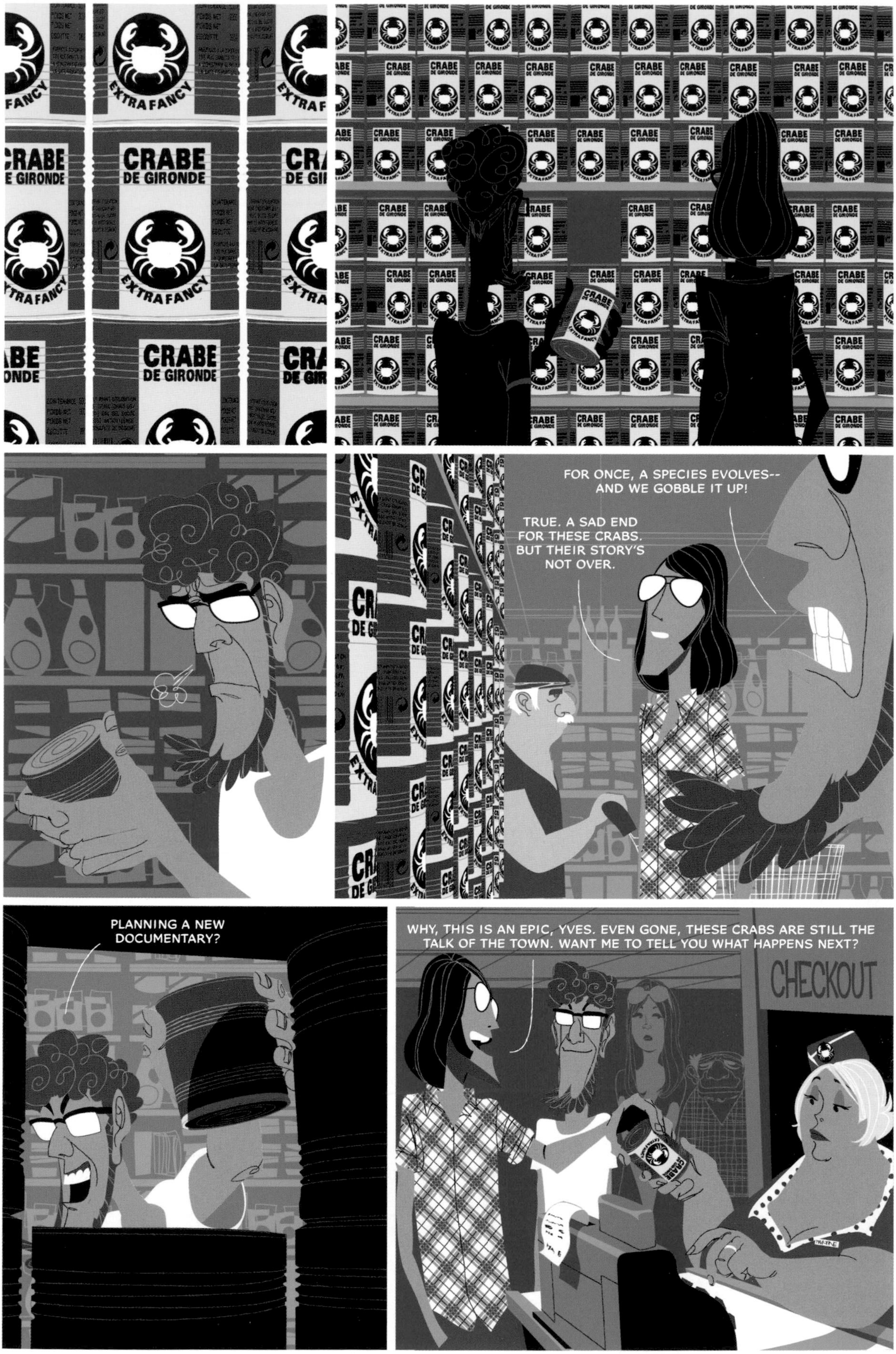
CRABE
DE GIRONDE
EXTRA FANCY
FOR ONCE, A SPECIES EVOLVES-- AND WE GOBBLE IT UP!
TRUE. A SAD END FOR THESE CRABS. BUT THEIR STORY'S NOT OVER.
PLANNING A NEW DOCUMENTARY?
WHY, THIS IS AN EPIC, YVES. EVEN GONE, THESE CRABS ARE STILL THE TALK OF THE TOWN. WANT ME TO TELL YOU WHAT HAPPENS NEXT?
CHECKOUT

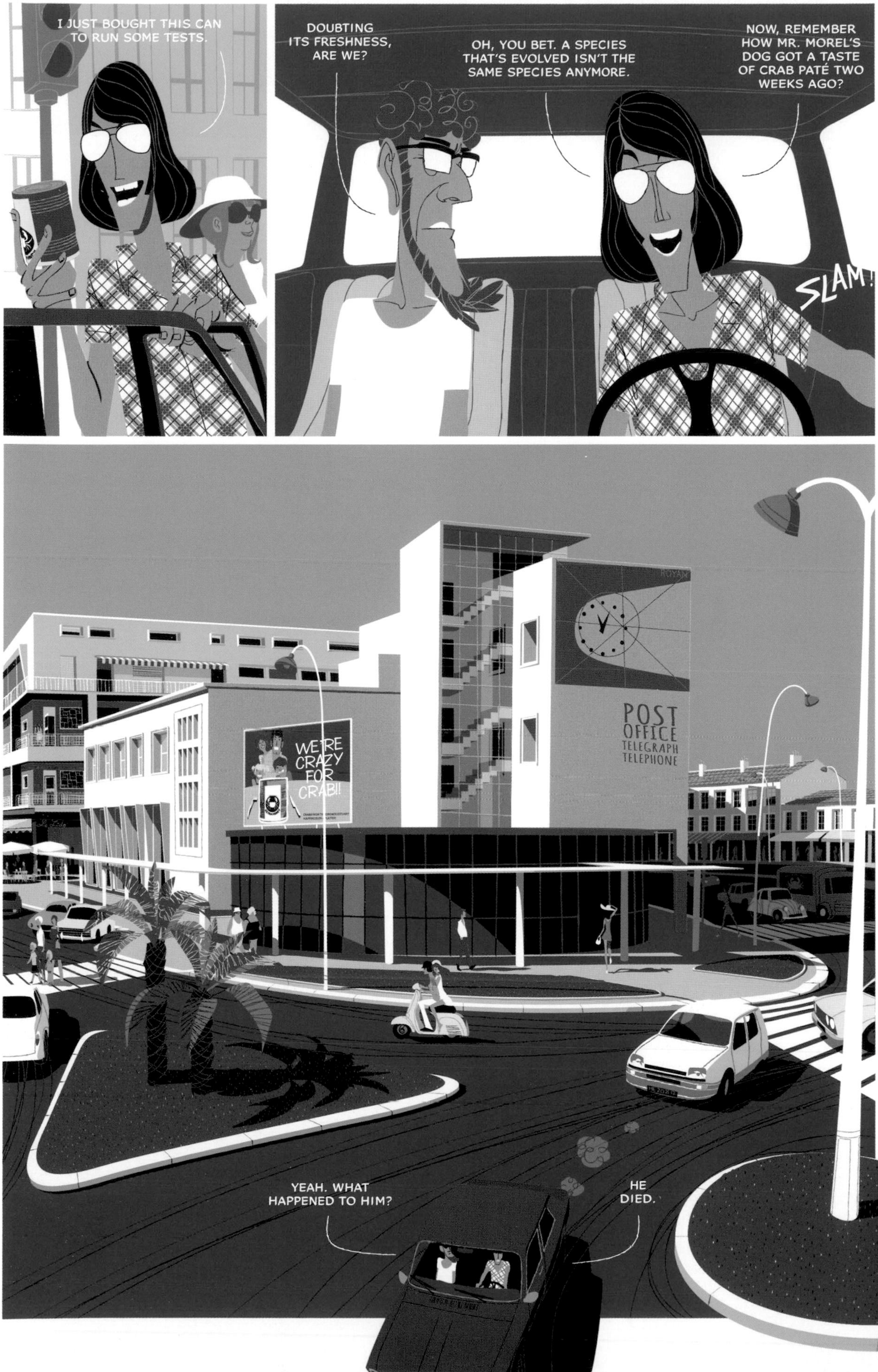
I JUST BOUGHT THIS CAN TO RUN SOME TESTS.
DOUBTING ITS FRESHNESS, ARE WE?
OH, YOU BET. A SPECIES THAT'S EVOLVED ISN'T THE SAME SPECIES ANYMORE.
NOW, REMEMBER HOW MR. MOREL'S DOG GOT A TASTE OF CRAB PATÉ TWO WEEKS AGO?
SLAM!
ROYAN
WE'RE CRAZY FOR CRAB!!
POST OFFICE TELEGRAPH TELEPHONE
YEAH. WHAT HAPPENED TO HIM?
HE DIED.

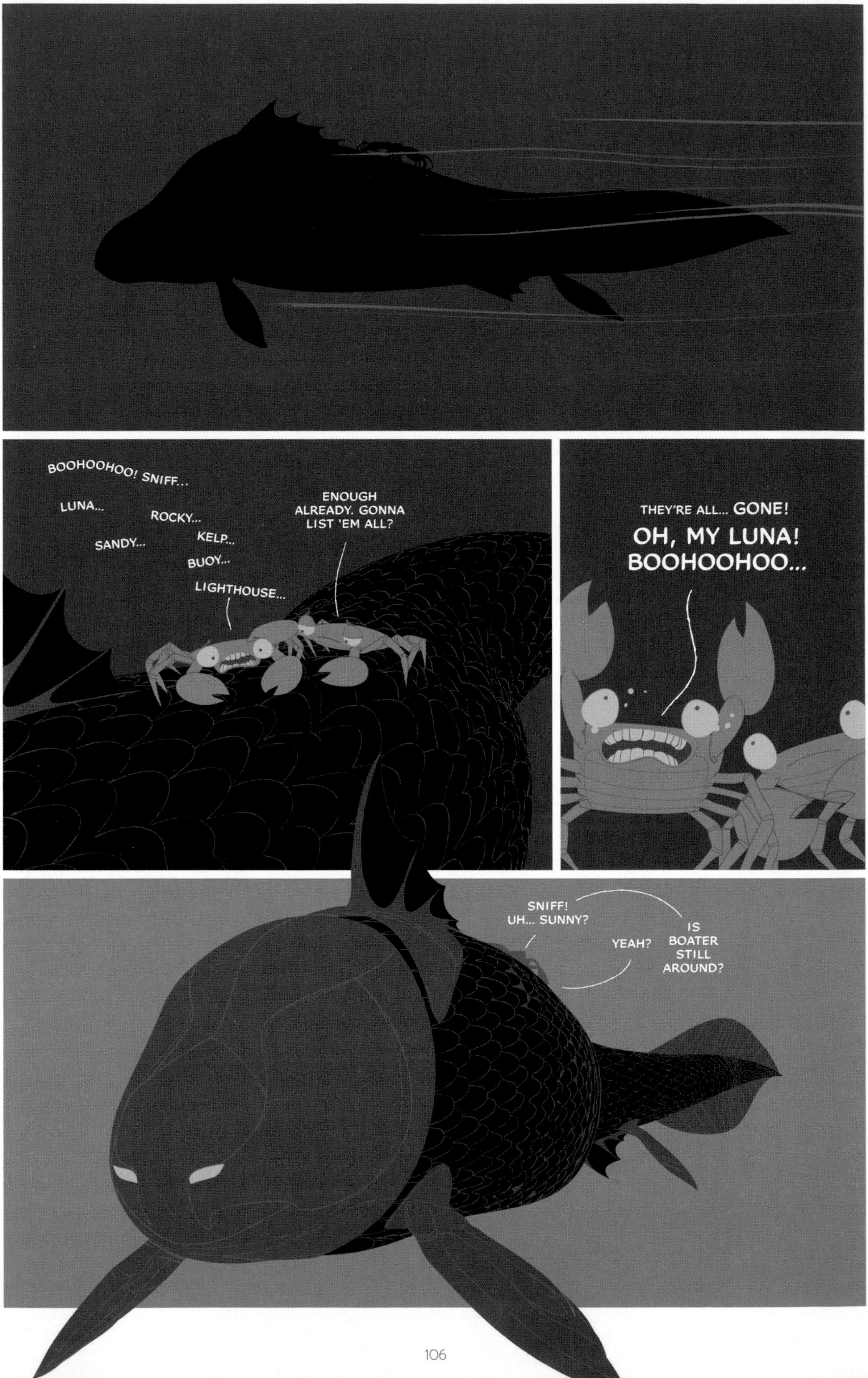
BOOHOOHOO! SNIFF...
LUNA...
ROCKY...
SANDY...
KELP...
BUOY...
LIGHTHOUSE...
ENOUGH ALREADY. GONNA LIST 'EM ALL?
THEY'RE ALL... GONE!
OH, MY LUNA! BOOHOOHOO...
SNIFF! UH... SUNNY?
YEAH?
IS BOATER STILL AROUND?

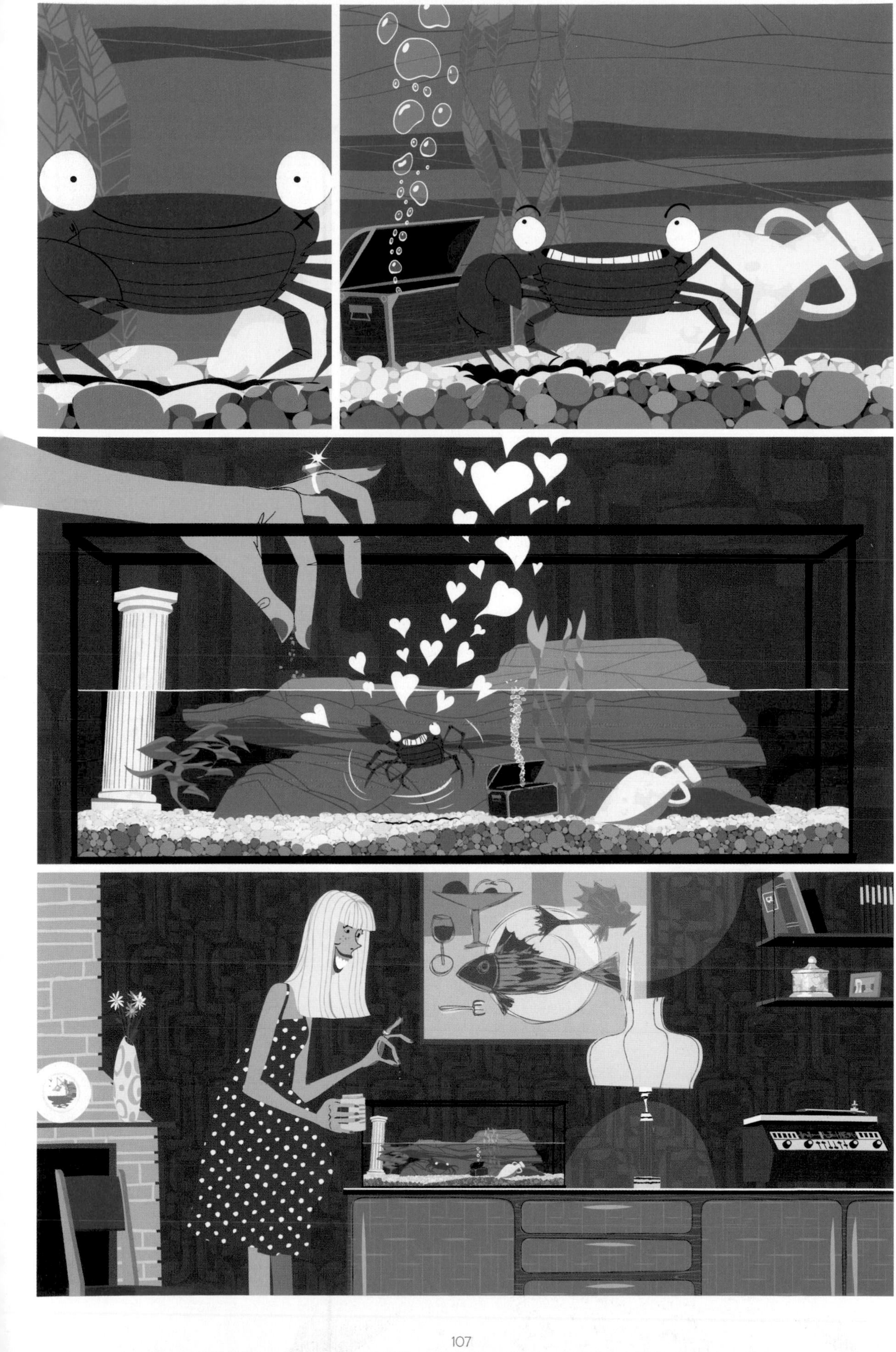

OK, CRABS!
END OF THE LINE!
I CAN'T GO UP ANY HIGHER. YOUR DUMB BEACH IS STRAIGHT AHEAD. FOLLOW THOSE ROCKS.
THANKS, ACHILLES.
I'M SORRY ABOUT YOUR PEOPLE, BOYS.
BUT I MUST SAY... YOU DISAPPOINTED ME.
I WAS BETTING ON YOU!

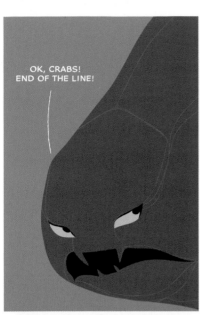

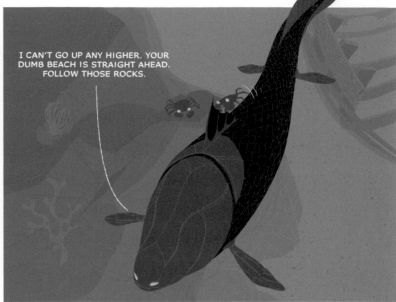

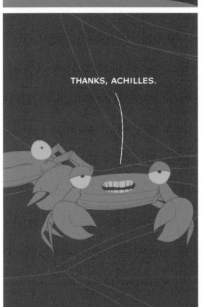

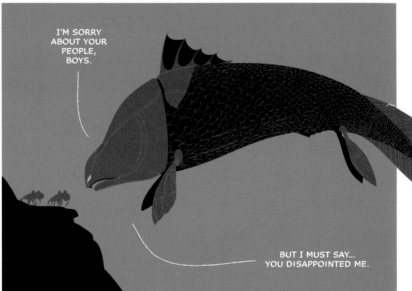

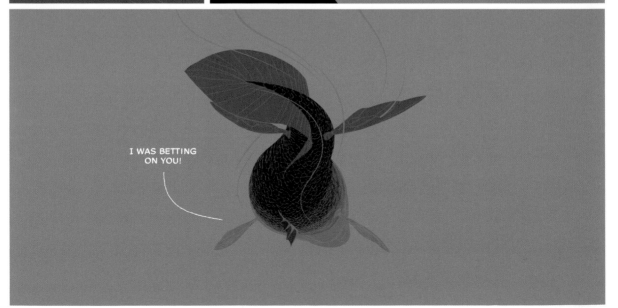

SUNNY!

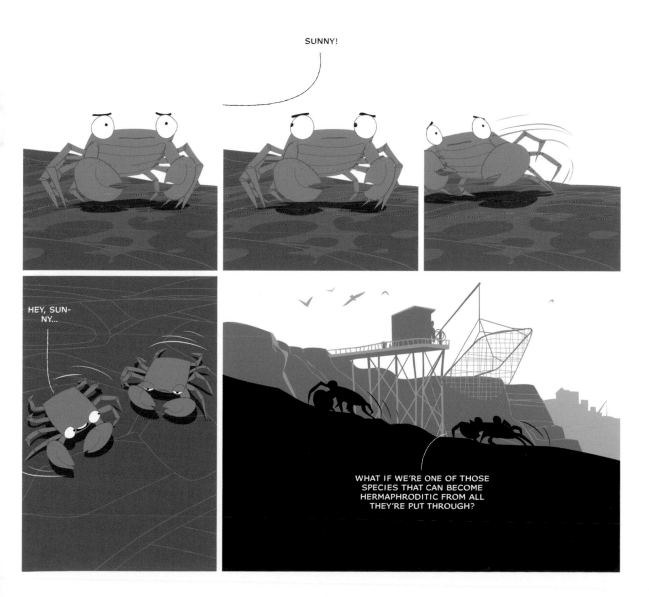

HEY, SUN-NY...

WHAT IF WE'RE ONE OF THOSE
SPECIES THAT CAN BECOME
HERMAPHRODITIC FROM ALL
THEY'RE PUT THROUGH?

IN WHICH CASE, WE COULD, UH... HAVE... KIDS?

TO PERPETUATE THE SPECIES...

UM...

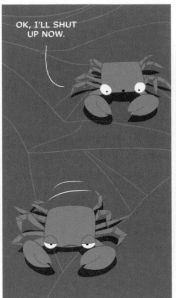

OK, I'LL SHUT UP NOW.

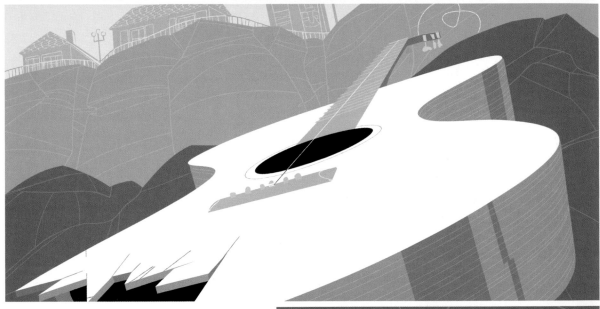

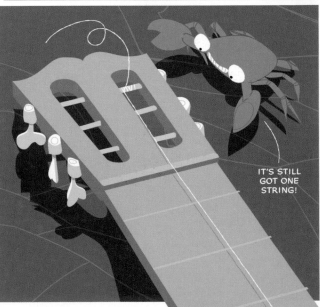

IT'S STILL GOT ONE STRING!

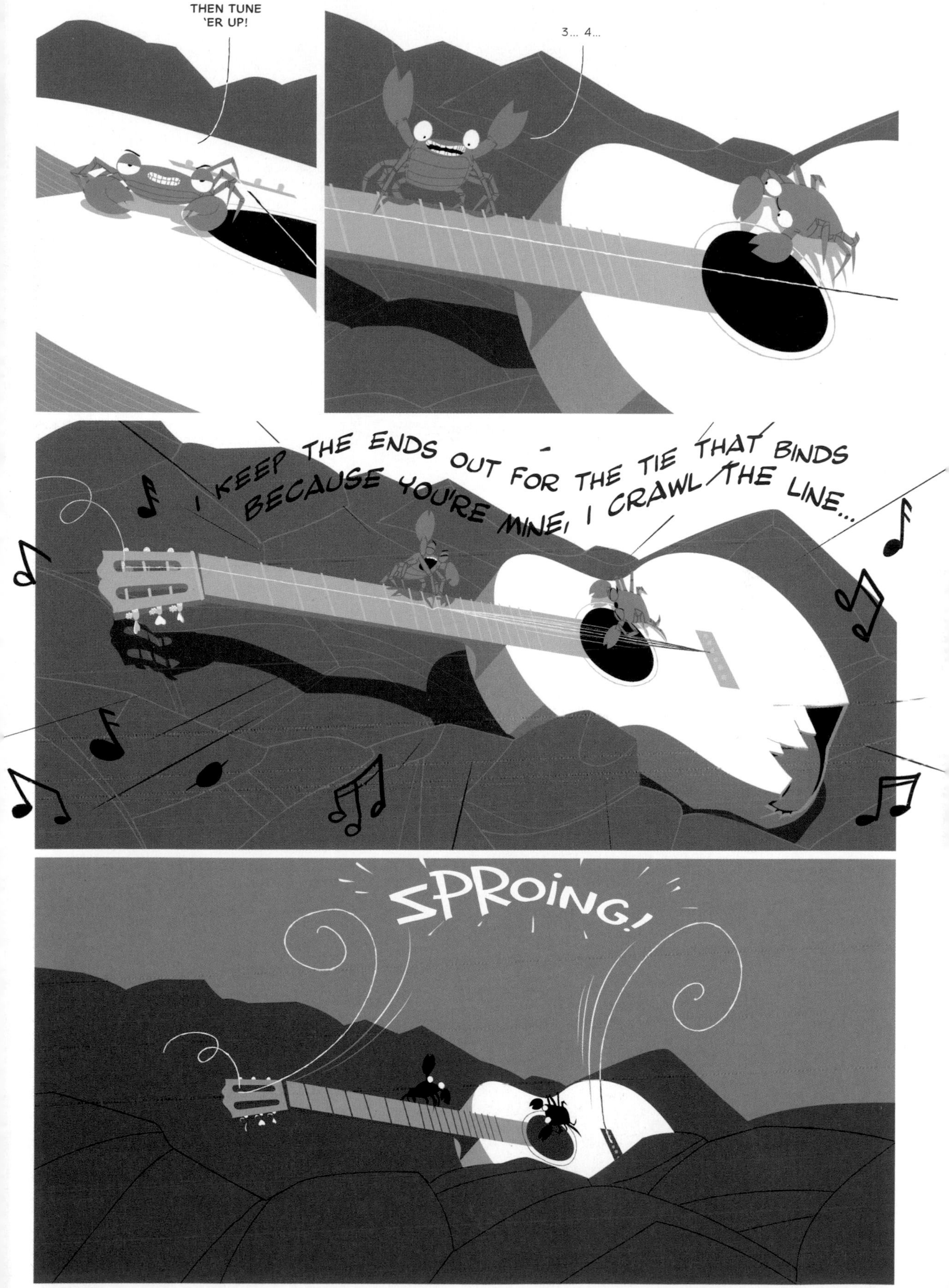
THEN TUNE 'ER UP!
3... 4...
I KEEP THE ENDS OUT FOR THE TIE THAT BINDS
BECAUSE YOU'RE MINE, I CRAWL THE LINE...
SPROING!

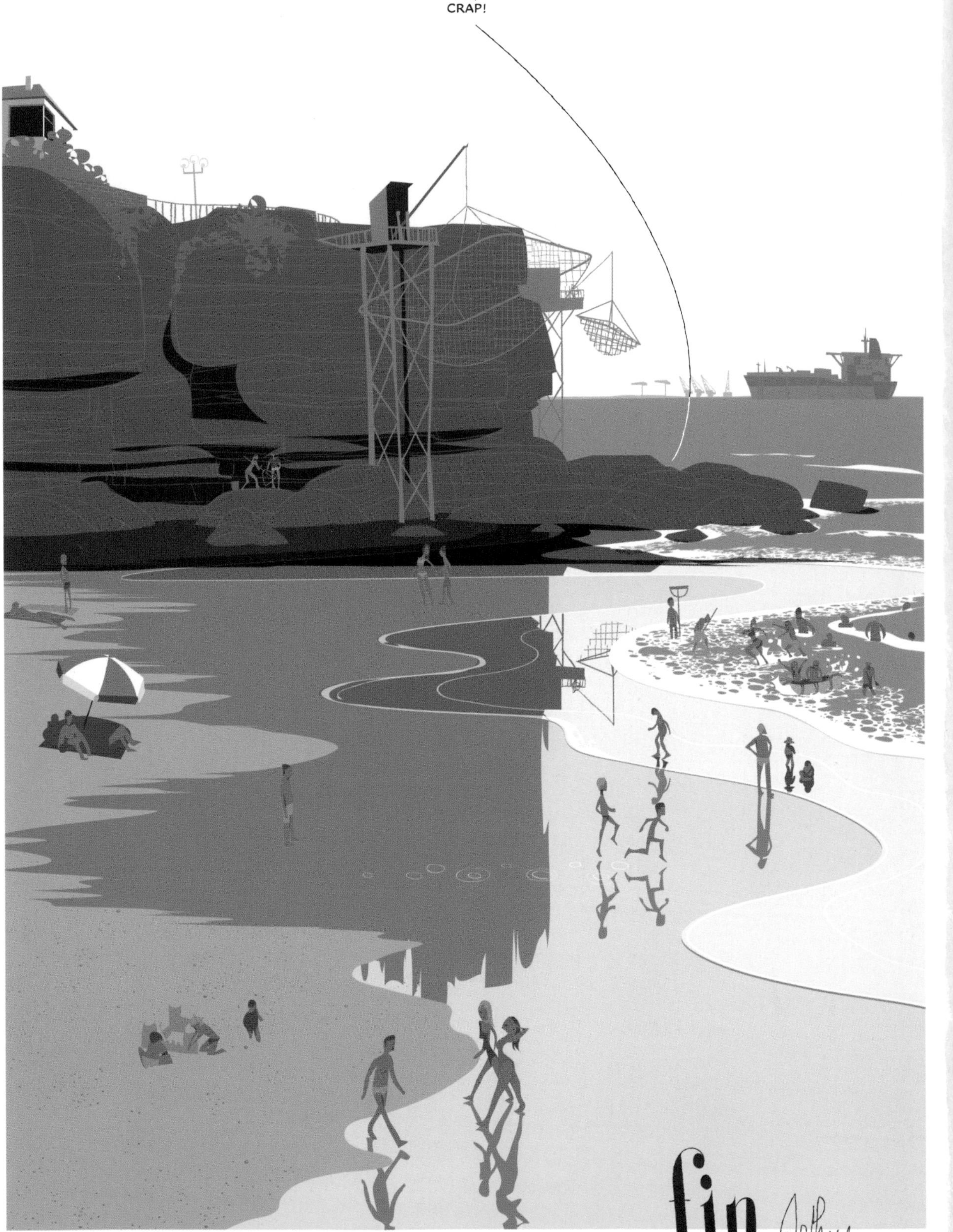
AH,
CRAP!
fin
Arthur de Pins
Août 201

ACKNOWLEDGEMENTS

To Jeremy who laid the first stone with his burst of enthusiasm and research grants, then went on to produce the short film *The Crab Revolution* in 2004, in what should have been a series of animated films. But ultimately became, through the magic of cinema…a graphic novel.

To my grandparents and parents who, every summer, took their family to the shores of the beautiful coast despite water where one can hardly see their feet.

To all the old regulars of the Pigeonnier beach, in particular Jean-Pierre, Linette, and Suzie.

To my mentors in the field of illustration: Edmond Kiraz, Miroslav Sasek, and the unrivaled "Sir" Richard Zielenkiewicz, a native of Royan who paid tribute to its architecture.

To my cousin, Erwan "Captain" Donnelly, the video reporter who was in love with the sea and who left us in 2005.

To my friends who have continued to encourage me by making me keep pictures of crabs from four corners of the globe. The trilogy is over, but nothing prevents you from continuing this tradition.

To Adeline and Didier who shaped this trilogy in good humor.

And finally, to the incomparable Clotilde Vu for his gaiety, his taste for beautiful books, and his "yes" to this project.

And of course, to all the crabs in the Gironde estuary that I fished as kid and whose destiny I have probably changed by releasing them a few meters further away.

Arthur De Pins

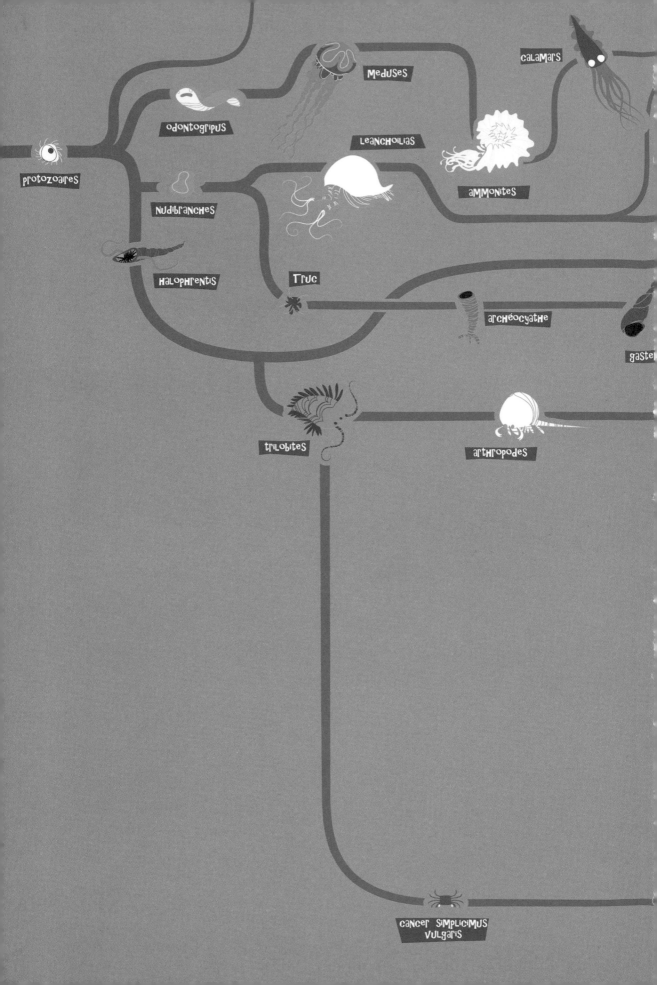

protozoaires

odontogripus

meduses

calamars

leanchoilias

nudibranches

ammonites

halophrentis

Truc

archéocyathe

gaster

trilobites

arthropodes

cancer simplicimus
vulgaris